AI and Bots in Everyday Life

Heiko Knödel · Dietmar Seipel

AI and Bots in Everyday Life

Understanding Artificial Intelligence and Using It for Business, Home & School

Springer

Heiko Knödel
efacon GmbH
Bad Vilbel, Germany

Dietmar Seipel
Institut für Informatik (Künstliche Intelligenz und Wissenssysteme)
Julius-Maximilians-Universität Würzburg
Würzburg, Bayern, Germany

ISBN 978-3-658-51143-2 ISBN 978-3-658-51144-9 (eBook)
https://doi.org/10.1007/978-3-658-51144-9

This book is a translation of the original German edition "KI und Bots im Alltag" by Heiko Knödel and Dietmar Seipel, published by Springer Fachmedien Wiesbaden GmbH in 2025. The translation was done with the help of an artificial intelligence machine translation tool. A subsequent human revision was done primarily in terms of content, so that the book will read stylistically differently from a conventional translation. Springer Nature works continuously to further the development of tools for the production of books and on the related technologies to support the authors.

This Springer imprint is published by the registered company Springer Fachmedien Wiesbaden GmbH, part of Springer Nature.
The registered company address is: Abraham-Lincoln-Str. 46, 65189 Wiesbaden, Germany

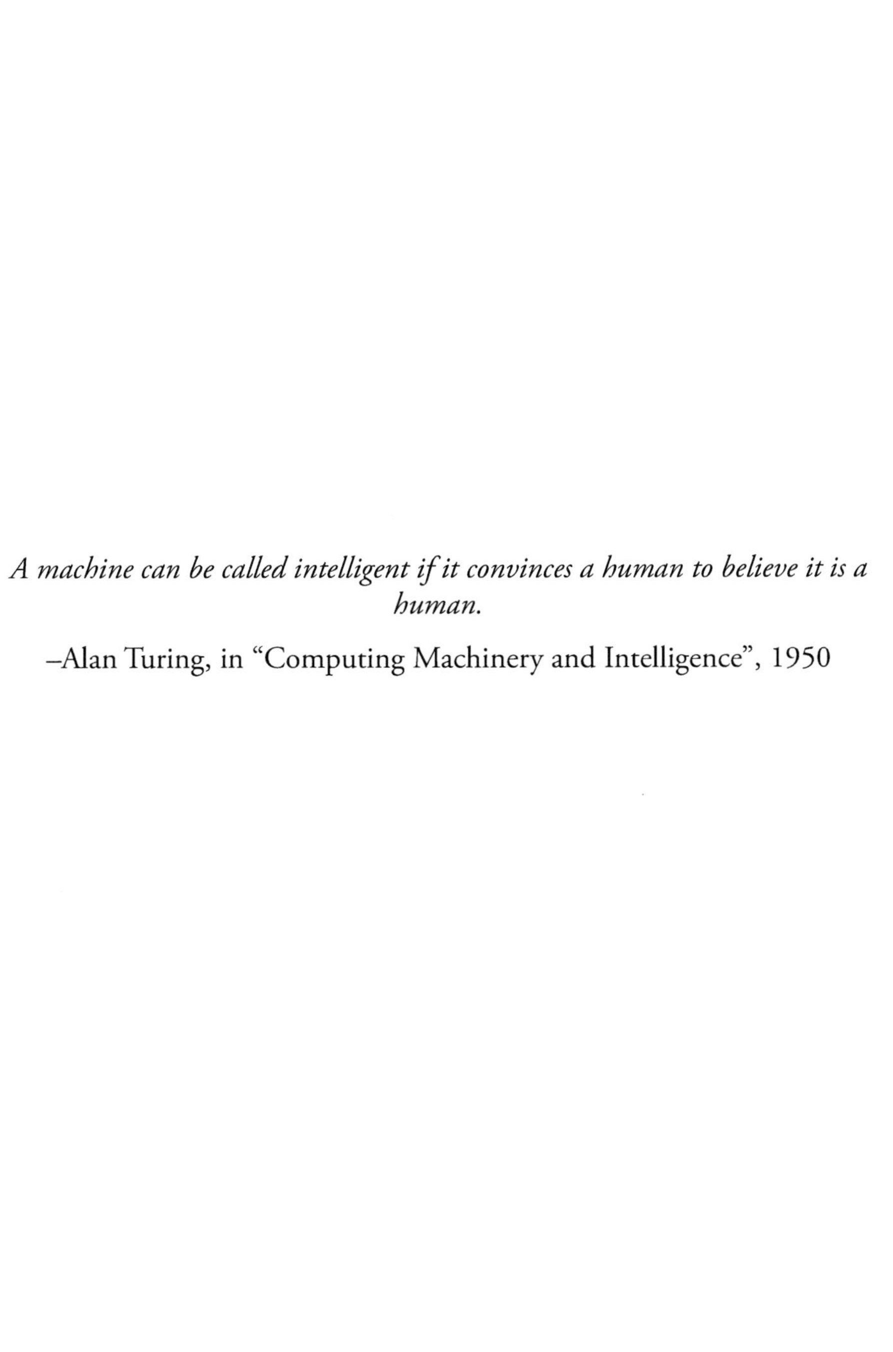

A machine can be called intelligent if it convinces a human to believe it is a human.

–Alan Turing, in "Computing Machinery and Intelligence", 1950

Preface by the Authors

We are entering a new era—one in which artificial intelligence is not only providing new tools, but fundamentally reshaping how we think, work, and create.

AI is no longer a promise for the future—it is reality. The speed at which AI technologies are advancing is breathtaking. What once emerged in researchers' laboratories is now widely used in businesses, classrooms, and even our everyday lives.

Artificial intelligence extends far beyond code and algorithms. It enables systems to learn, interpret, and interact with their environment. Large language models can process complex information, while logic-based systems support structured reasoning and decision-making. The ability to extract knowledge, that is, the automatic acquisition of knowledge, is becoming increasingly sophisticated, allowing bots and AI systems to increasingly function as effective partners in everyday life. In businesses, intelligent systems optimize processes and make data-driven decisions. In schools, smart tutor bots support students and teachers. And in our homes, digital assistants and autonomous devices take on tasks that would have seemed unthinkable just a few years ago.

With all these developments, however, challenges are also growing—ethical questions, economic upheavals, and the necessity to act with responsibility and foresight. How far can and do we want to trust machines? What role does the human play in a world where AI not only automates processes but also influences decisions?

The book 'AI and Bots in Everyday Life: Understanding Artificial Intelligence and Using It for Business, Home & School' is a unique blend of in-depth expertise and accessible presentation, making the topic of Artificial Intelligence (AI) tangible for a broad audience of beginners through current practical applications. We convey the fundamentals of AI without descending into technical jargon, while also highlighting its diverse applications in everyday life. Particularly noteworthy is our chapter on ethics and the future of AI, which encourages critical reflection and mirrors current debates. With our book, we offer a valuable resource for readers seeking both an overview and a deeper understanding of AI.

We shed light on what is often perceived as an abstract field of Artificial Intelligence. Our approach combines humorous storytelling with precise, expert information to appeal to a wide range of readers. The book is carefully structured to guide readers from fundamental concepts to advanced applications and ethical considerations. Through real-world examples and practical scenarios, we demonstrate how profoundly AI influences and shapes our daily lives. Our goal is to bridge the gap between the technical world of AI and everyday understanding, in order to provide a comprehensive and balanced picture of this revolutionary technology.

This book is suitable for entrepreneurs who are particularly interested in the chapters on organizing AI within a company (Chap. 2), the distinction and application of large language models for generative AI (Chap. 3), as well as AI in everyday work (Chap. 4). However, the book is also suitable for students and teachers who are keen to engage with the fundamentals and history of AI (Chap. 1), large language models and their applications (Chap. 2), and the benefits and added value of AI at school and at home (Chap. 5). For technology enthusiasts and possibly scientists, the content on decision trees (Chap. 6), knowledge extraction (Chap. 7), and knowledge-based systems and logic programming (Chap. 8) will likely be the most interesting. For all those interested in the future and possible scenarios and stories from the future, the opportunities, risks, and ethics of AI (Chap. 9) and the stories on trends and the future of AI (Chap. 10) will hopefully provide an exciting contribution and inspiration.

This book is an invitation to engage with the possibilities and limitations of AI. It is not only about technology, but also about the future we will shape together. At the same time, it also explores future developments: What developments await us? Which ethical and societal questions must we address?

One thing is certain: The most exciting question is not what machines can do, but what we humans want to achieve in harmony with technology.

Inclusive and respectful language is important to us. To improve readability when referring to people and personal nouns, we have largely avoided double designations and gendered terms, and use the generic masculine form in this book. Of course, all genders are always equally intended.

Heiko Knödel
Dietmar Seipel

Acknowledgment

This book would not have been possible without the support and inspiration that have accompanied us on our journey.

The authors Heiko Knödel and Dietmar Seipel would like to thank their families for their patience and understanding—especially their wives Phoudida Knödel and Claire Huang: You have been our constant source of support and strength. Your unwavering faith in us, your patience, and your love have always reminded us why we walk this path. You have shown us that true inspiration often begins right at our own doorstep. And heartfelt thanks also to Heiko's children Samira and Bennet, who sketched a few scenes with pictures.

Special thanks also go to the people who have shaped us along our life's journey—mentors, companions, and inspiring individuals who have shared their wisdom, experiences, and encouraged us to pursue ambitious ideas. Your words and deeds resonate throughout this book, and for that we are infinitely grateful to you.

We are glad that we never stopped believing in our vision. Tireless curiosity has always driven us forward. The reminder that we can all be our own mentor teaches us to listen to our inner voice.

We dedicate this book to all those who have the courage to inspire themselves and others. You are the driving force behind everything we can create together.

Understanding Artificial Intelligence and Using It for Business, School & Everyday Life

In a world increasingly shaped by technology, artificial intelligence (AI) is often perceived as complex or difficult to access. Yet AI is no longer limited to large technology companies, research institutes, and scientists; it is a practical system that affects and influences many aspects of everyday life. The question is no longer whether we will use AI, but how effectively and responsibly we choose to apply it. In this book, we break down the complexity of AI and make it understandable for everyone—from theory to practical application.

The objective of the two co-authors is to bring AI closer to readers in Germany. Many *practical use cases* demonstrate the *advantages* and *opportunities* of AI. Smaller theoretical sections—especially on knowledge-based systems—are intended to provide deeper insights into AI in some places (which, from a research perspective, still only scratches the surface).

One should also pay attention to *risks* and *ethics*, point them out, or provide assistance in recognizing, for example, fake videos. However, the risks do not simply disappear if one closes their eyes and avoids engaging with AI. This sometimes appears to be the case among the population in Germany. We aim to counteract this with education and transparency, to ensure continued technological competitiveness.

Subfields of AI and Historical Development

Artificial intelligence can broadly be divided into two main approaches: symbolic and subsymbolic methods. *Symbolic methods* model central human cognitive abilities such as logic, deduction, and planning in computers, and are often knowledge-based. These methods rely on clearly defined mathematical rules. Their transparency—through logical reasoning steps—helps address key challenges in digitalization. In addition, more recently, *sub-symbolic methods* attempt to learn a model of a process (e.g., an optimal action for a robot or the classification of sensor data) from training data (statistically) using machine learning and deep learning. Neural networks are often used for this purpose, which aim to replicate the functioning of the human brain. In biological systems, neurons communicate through complex signal transmission processes. Artificial neural networks are inspired by this principle and model simplified versions of these interactions.

The *historical development* of AI dates back to the early 20th century, long before the term itself was introduced. Foundational work in mathematical logic by researchers such as *David Hilbert* and *Kurt Gödel established the basis for formal knowledge representation.* Around 1900, knowledge representation using logical formulas of varying complexity (propositional and predicate logic) was formalized. This knowledge allowed logical conclusions to be derived using formal inference methods (inference, derivation). In 1950, the famous British computer scientist *Alan Turing* proposed testing whether a machine exhibits intelligent behavior indistinguishable from that of a human (Turing Test). In 1956, many scientists at the first AI workshop at Dartmouth College, USA, expected that machines could reach human-level intelligence within a generation. Although it took a bit longer, some systems have demonstrated behavior that resembles passing the Turing Test in specific contexts, in recent years—and the actual Turing Test, in the sense of acting in a human-like manner permanently, robustly, and in every everyday situation, could, according to current estimates, be passed before 2040. Robots with intelligent behavior could become possible in the future.

By 2090, even super-intelligent, self-optimizing beings could become possible.

The *most recent practical developments* in AI can be followed in the media; for example, AI successes in quiz shows like Jeopardy (2011), victories against the world's best players in board games such as chess (1997) or Go (2016), self-driving cars (beginning in 1968), or chatbots like ChatGPT (2022). The annual IJCAI conferences (International Joint Conferences on AI) provide overviews of the most important scientific findings in AI; recently, research in AI has been supported by large amounts of government funding.

Summary

Part I (Development of AI – From Turing to Large Language Models) provides an introduction to the *fundamentals and history* of AI (Chap. 1) as well as to *AI in everyday work* (Chap. 2). Following an initial boom in the mid-1980s, investments in AI models and algorithms declined significantly as personal computers became commonplace in companies and almost every household. For some time now, AI has once again become broadly interesting, as the computing power—doubling approximately every nine months according to Moore's Law—now provides the capacity to analyze big data in real time. Language models (LLMs, Chap. 3) such as ChatGPT have existed for several years, but until recently were mainly used internally by individual companies for process workflows, early warning systems, and predictive analytics.

Part II (Current Use Cases) presents the trend toward specialization and its benefits for companies in the *world of work* (Chap. 4). We describe the progress enabled by the use of AI agents, which facilitate work and allow standard processes to be automated in an efficient and scalable way, thus helping to counteract the shortage of skilled workers. AI avatars are increasingly playing an important role in explainer videos as well as in knowledge transfer and addressing questions. The baby boomer generation will soon retire; their knowledge and experience can be captured in documents and videos and passed on to younger generations using AI-supported methods. A wide range of *AI tools and use cases* is considered: in civil and structural engineering, the automotive industry, autonomous robots, and digital twins. Next, the book explores *AI in schools and at home* (Chap. 5). In this chapter, it discusses how AI is already integrated into education, both as a learning tool for students and as a support system for teachers. In addition, it explores emerging trends in smart homes, household robotics, and future human–machine interactions. On the one hand, AI is already part of everyday life in many places, and therefore school graduates should also have a solid basic knowledge of AI. On the other hand, AI is used by students for homework, term papers, and presentations, as well as by teachers for creating teaching materials, lesson content, and exams.

Part III (Symbolic AI) first demonstrates the use and added value of decision trees, which can easily model and visualize hierarchically structured decision processes (Chap. 6). They make it possible to classify data or make predictions based on rules by representing decisions in a clear, interpretable tree structure. Next, AI for knowledge extraction is considered. These methods are over a hundred years old. The theoretical foundations of knowledge-based AI have been very well developed. As an example, we will get to know logic programming based on these foundations. Recently, a *hybrid approach* often combines sub-symbolic and symbolic AI, such as knowledge-based systems; there are different categories depending on the extent to which each approach is represented.

Part IV (Trends, Ethics, and the Future of AI) addresses ethics as well as *current trends* and the *future* of AI. The use and benefits of AI bring us many conveniences and improvements. AI is making its way into many areas of life—from medicine and business to entertainment. However, this rapid development is also accompanied by significant dangers and ethical issues, which we highlight here and which we must not ignore (Chap. 9). AI scenarios, a story from the future, a look at the future of AI itself, as well as the pursuit of a superintelligence that surpasses humanity, are considered as the final technical part of the book (Chap. 10).

In the appendix you will find the bibliography, the list of figures, and the list of tables. An index for quickly locating technical terms and important elements, as well as a brief biography of the two authors, complete the book.

Contents

About the Authors

Heiko Knödel understands progress. As early as the 1990s, the computer science graduate was digitizing processes while others were still stacking paper. Today, he leads a consulting and seminar company where he combines artificial intelligence, leadership, and mindset—a symbiosis of technology and human growth.

He has worked in responsible leadership and project positions for major companies such as Deutsche Bank, Porsche, BMW, and Merck.

His areas of expertise include artificial intelligence, digitalization, change and innovation management, process optimization, leadership, and mindset. He shares his knowledge as a mentor, coach, seminar leader, and speaker—clear, practical, and inspiring.

As an author, he sets impulses. His book *"Kita 4.0 – Simply Digital" (original title: "Kita 4.0 – einfach digital")* became a bestseller in several categories during the 2023 Frankfurt Book Fair.

Knödel is not a theorist. He thinks, designs, transforms. With empathy, intercultural competence, and the ability to inspire people. Anyone who experiences him leaves wiser and more motivated.

Dietmar Seipel has been a university professor for databases, knowledge-based systems, and logic programming at the University of Würzburg since 1995.

His field of work in knowledge-based systems belongs to AI. For many years, he has been the spokesperson for the Society for Logical Programming GLP e. V. in German-speaking countries. Within the German AI community, he serves on the board of the specialist group for declarative programming. In 2023, he was co-chairman of the AI conference in Berlin.

In this book, he wrote the chapter on knowledge-based systems and logic programming. He was also able to contribute to the introductory section on the fundamentals and history of AI.

List of Figures

List of Tables

Part I

Development of AI—from Turing to Large Language Models

1

Fundamentals and History of AI

Contents

Let's start with the basics. What is AI, anyway? We demystify the term by breaking it down into its fundamental components: algorithms, machine learning (ML), neural networks, and knowledge-based systems (KBS). This chapter makes it clear that AI is not just a distant vision of the future, but already a part of our everyday lives. Fig. 1.1 shows the Lego figures EVE and WALL-E as charming representatives of artificial intelligence and emotional robotics (Fig. 1.1).

Artificial intelligence (AI) is one of the most fascinating and revolutionary technologies of our time. AI refers to the ability of computers or machines to imitate human intelligence. This includes performing tasks that typically require human intelligence, such as learning,

H. Knödel and D. Seipel, *AI and Bots in Everyday Life*,
https://doi.org/10.1007/978-3-658-51144-9_1

Fig. 1.1 Photo of the Lego figures EVE and WALL-E

problem-solving, and decision-making. Whether you have a positive attitude toward AI or want to keep it out of your life for as long as possible, AI is already here and will continue to spread. AI has the potential to change virtually every aspect of our daily lives, just as computers entered nearly every household in the 1990s. Or as smartphones became widespread. Many people who long said they didn't need one now own one.

1.1 Symbolic and Subsymbolic AI

The field of AI distinguishes between symbolic and subsymbolic methods. Symbolic AI works with explicit rules and logical structures to represent knowledge and solve problems, similar to traditional databases. Knowledge-based symbolic methods support core human cognitive abilities through logic. Subsymbolic AI, on the other hand, uses pattern recognition and learning methods, as in neural networks, to tackle tasks through statistical learning and data processing. Thanks to increasing computing power and the availability of vast amounts of knowledge on the internet, subsymbolic approaches such as machine learning have become very popular and successful today. Hybrid approaches attempt to combine the advantages of both types of methods.

Symbolic AI
Symbolic AI is based on explicit rules and logical structures represented by human-readable symbols. It works with knowledge that is stored in the form of symbols and processed according to fixed rules. In this approach, knowledge is deliberately encoded by humans, for example through algorithms, knowledge bases, or decision trees.

An example of symbolic AI is *expert systems*. These are systems based on predefined rules, such as medical diagnostic systems. Another example is *logic-based expert systems*. These include Prolog programs or applications that use predicate logic. And another, somewhat better-known example is *first-generation chess programs*, which operated using *search algorithms* and fixed strategies.

The advantages of symbolic AI lie in its *transparency* and *controllability*. Transparency means that decisions are traceable and explainable. Controllability means that humans can directly change or extend the rules.

The disadvantages become apparent in the face of uncertain events. It is difficult to deal with *uncertainties*, incomplete information, or complexly structured data. In addition, *flexibility* and *scalability* are limited.

A classic example of symbolic AI is the navigation system in a car. Here, the so-called Iterative Deepening Search (*IDS*) is used to efficiently search possible routes. The optimal route is first calculated with a shallow depth (i.e., the fastest connections, such as highways, between two points are analyzed first). The calculation is then gradually extended until the optimal route is found. This saves memory, works relatively quickly and efficiently, and ensures a complete search, especially in complex road networks where the target distance is initially unknown.

Figure 1.2 shows an example of an algorithm for iterative deepening search without AI. In this simple example, the algorithm searches for the way out of the maze by always keeping to the right, which sounds like a simple, pragmatic, and perfect solution. However, this example already clearly shows that the algorithm would never find the exit if there were an open loop in the maze—for instance, if the vertical partition at the bottom center, which we have drawn in green for

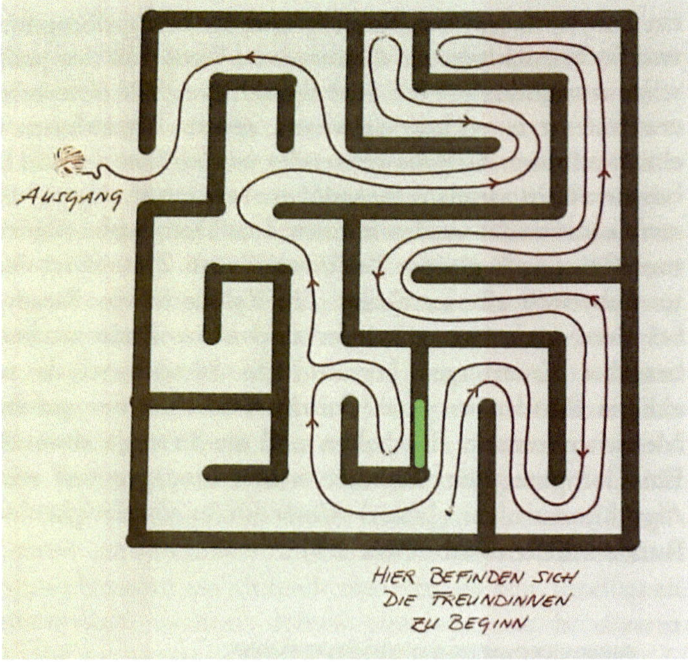

Fig. 1.2 Finding the way out of the maze using the depth-first search algorithm (Kersting et al., 2019)

illustration, did not exist—because then the algorithm would move in circles indefinitely.

Subsymbolic AI

Subsymbolic AI works with data-driven models in which processing is not based on explicit rules, but on numerical representations. Here, models learn patterns, relationships, and functions directly from data, without explicit rules being defined.

An example of subsymbolic AI is *neural networks*. This includes deep learning models such as *convolutional neural networks (CNNs)* or *transformer* architectures. Another example is *reinforcement learning*. Here, algorithms such as AlphaGo are used, which learn through trial and error. In addition, *speech recognition* and *image processing* also fall within the domain of subsymbolic AI.

The advantages lie in their *performance* with large, complex, and unstructured data, as well as their *adaptability* to new data through learning algorithms. The disadvantages, on the one hand, are the *black-box nature* of these systems, as decisions are difficult to trace. On the other hand, there is a strong *dependence on data*, since large amounts of training data are required.

Comparison of Approaches

Table 1.1 provides an overview of the differences between symbolic and subsymbolic AI in terms of their functioning, strengths, and areas of application. (See Table 1.1)

Table 1.1 Comparison of symbolic and subsymbolic AI

Aspect	Symbolic AI	Subsymbolic AI
Approach	Rule-based, explicit	Data-driven, implicit
Data requirements	Low	High
Explainability	High	Low
Areas of application	Structured problems	Complex pattern recognition
Flexibility	Limited	High

Hybrid Approaches

In modern AI research, *hybrid approaches* are often intended to combine the strengths of both paradigms. *Neuro-symbolic AI* uses symbolic logic to make the knowledge in neural networks interpretable, or subsymbolic AI to train symbolic systems more efficiently. For example, IBM Watson combines rule-based systems with machine learning. Symbolic and subsymbolic AI complement each other and together are key to advances in artificial intelligence.

Frequently, inputs and outputs are processed symbolically, while the actual computation is performed by neural networks. In contrast, AlphaGo, AlphaZero, and current approaches for autonomous vehicles embed neural pattern recognition within a symbolic problem solver. Conversely, symbolic reasoning can be incorporated into a neural machine. In Deep Learning for Symbolic Mathematics, symbolic rules are "compiled away" through training. In neuro-symbolic concept learning, there is ultimately a transition from a neural system to symbolic reasoning.

1.2 Subtypes of AI

There are many different subtypes of AI. In this section, we would like to highlight what we consider to be the most important subtypes. (See Fig. 1.3)

We would also like to point out that the subtypes of AI are considered orthogonal to symbolic and subsymbolic AI. That is, it is a completely different perspective, similar to comparing objects by weight or size—there is no necessary correlation here either.

Machine Learning (ML) uses algorithms that learn rules, apply them, and make decisions based on them. The decision-making process can also be trained and can learn autonomously, for example when new, unknown data is analyzed and checked for certain patterns and features. This is where decision trees come into play. These are a versatile machine learning method that model and visualize hierarchically structured decision-making processes. They make it possible to classify data

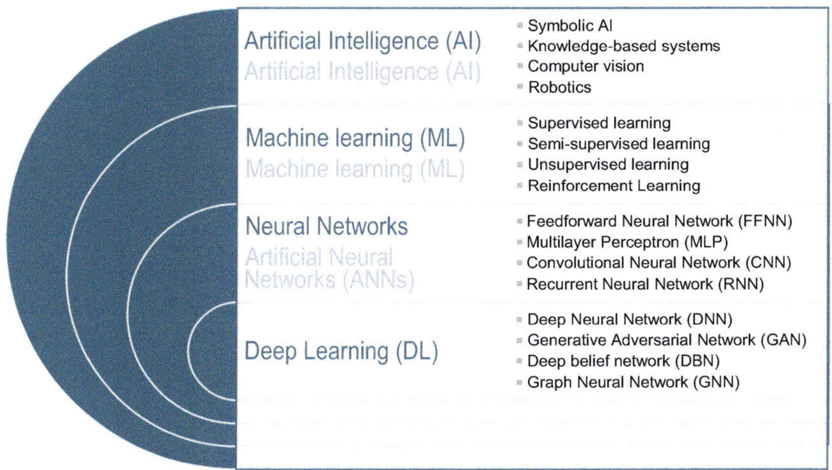

Fig. 1.3 Overview of the subtypes of AI (Medicine, 2022)

or make predictions based on rules by representing decisions in a clear, interpretable tree structure.

AI aims to enable machines to perform tasks that require artificial intelligence, such as recognizing speech, making decisions, or understanding texts. The key to this is machine learning, a subfield of AI that uses algorithms to identify patterns in data, learn from them, and make decisions or predictions based on this, often with an accuracy that humans cannot match.

In machine learning, algorithms are fed large amounts of data and trained to perform specific tasks by learning from examples. The learning process can be supervised, unsupervised, or reinforced, depending on how the data is presented and how feedback is provided. *"Even more astonishing than the breadth of applications of machine learning is that it's the same algorithms doing all of these different things. Outside of machine learning, if you have two different problems to solve, you need to write two different programs."*[1] (Domingos, The Master Algorithm, 2015).

[1] Original quote in English: *"Even more astonishing than the breadth of applications of machine learning is that it's the same algorithms doing all of these different things. Outside of machine learning, if you have two different problems to solve, you need to write two different programs."*

The ability to learn from experience and adapt without being explicitly programmed is what makes AI algorithms so powerful. They can recognize patterns in data that are invisible to the human eye, and they can be improved over time by receiving more data and feedback. This continuous improvement and adaptability are at the heart of every AI system.

Artificial neural networks are loosely inspired by the biological networks in the brains of mammals. Just as in the human brain, for example, nerve cells are interconnected via synapses, various artificial neurons and their connections form a network that can be used for computations. Each artificial neuron receives a signal, processes it, and, if necessary, passes it on to the next artificial neuron.

Neural networks learn to solve tasks without being explicitly programmed to do so. In image recognition, for example, a neural network can independently learn whether a car is visible in an image, provided it has previously been fed with sample images labeled with the features car/no car. The neural network does not need to know that a car has four wheels and drives on the road. It independently learns the attributes that define a car in images. (Wennker, 2020).

Deep Learning (DL) is a subgroup of ML. It typically involves the use of Artificial Neural Networks (ANNs), which are organized into multiple layers to mimic the human brain as closely as possible and arrive at the correct conclusions. DL is frequently used to identify patterns and relationships in large datasets. Through backpropagation and optimizations, the system continuously learns and helps reduce errors. DL is well suited for classification, regression calculation, or predictions. Common application areas include image recognition, speech processing, autonomous driving, and medical diagnostics.

Computer Vision (CV) is the subfield of AI that recognizes and interprets images, or can extract relevant information from an image. This is used, for example, in the identification and classification of animals and plants.

Knowledge-based systems (KBS) play a central role in AI and are one of the oldest and most important approaches in this field. They can represent explicit knowledge and draw inferences from it to find solutions and make decisions. Knowledge-based systems make it possible to represent expert knowledge in a structured and formal way, for example in the form of rules, facts, ontologies, knowledge graphs, or semantic networks. They provide a solid foundation for many AI applications that require structured knowledge, decision justification, and "logical inference" (a technical term in computer science referring to a logical conclusion drawn based on knowledge and rules), and they are increasingly used in combination with other approaches such as machine learning. Examples include expert systems that provide medical diagnoses based on symptoms and diseases, or systems for technical troubleshooting. A major advantage of knowledge-based systems is their ability to provide explanations for decisions. In contrast to some modern "black box" machine learning approaches such as neural networks, they are particularly useful when traceability is important, for example in medicine and law.

In modern AI applications, knowledge-based systems are often combined with machine learning.

Fuzzy Logic (FL) is used to solve complex problems using non-binary values that cannot be addressed by classical logic. An example from everyday life is the regulation of room temperature by heating systems and air conditioners. Fuzzy logic makes it possible to keep the temperature as constant as possible. For example, if a room temperature of 22 degrees Celsius is desired, a conventional heater would heat at full power, i.e., 100%, at 21 degrees and then switch off at 22 degrees, which, due to residual heating, would result in a temperature of around 24 or 25 degrees Celsius. Thus, before the use of fuzzy logic, the room temperature fluctuated constantly. Fuzzy logic compares the current room temperature with the target temperature and reduces the heating power as the target temperature is approached. That is, when reaching 21.5 degrees Celsius, the heating power is, for example, reduced to 25% to approach the target temperature as gently as possible. Game controllers and joysticks also often use fuzzy logic.

Natural Language Processing (NLP) is the area of AI that deals with understanding natural language and speech patterns. The best-known example of this is ChatGPT. Thanks to smart algorithms in the background, NLP is the interface between humans and machines, enabling computers to understand, interpret, and meaningfully process language.

From chatbots to automatic translations to voice assistants—NLP ensures that technology speaks our language. It combines linguistics with AI methods such as machine learning to analyze texts, recognize patterns, and generate responses.

1.3 Historical Development

Long before the term Artificial Intelligence (AI) was coined, the development of *mathematical logic* began in the 20th century with researchers such as David Hilbert and Kurt Gödel. Around 1900, *knowledge representation* using logical formulas of varying complexity (propositional and predicate logic) was formalized. *Inferences* from knowledge could be drawn using logical calculi (inference, derivation).

> *Those who search for methods without having a defined problem in mind usually search in vain.*

This quote comes from David Hilbert's famous speech "Mathematical Problems," which he delivered on August 8, 1900, at the International Congress of Mathematicians in Paris. In this speech, Hilbert presented 23 unsolved problems that significantly influenced mathematical research in the 20th century. The quoted statement emphasizes the importance of focusing on concrete problems rather than aimlessly searching for general methods.

A more precise concept of AI emerged through Alan Turing in the 1950s. He dealt with the outcome of AI and how it should be considered in comparison to the natural intelligence of humans.

Alan Turing
In the following, we will take a closer look at the famous British computer scientist and logician *Alan Turing* (6/23/1912–6/7/1954) and the *Turing Test*. In 1950, he proposed testing whether a machine exhibits intelligent behavior indistinguishable from that of a human (Turing Test). In 1956, many scientists at the first AI workshop at Dartmouth College, USA, hoped that within a generation there would be machines

as intelligent as humans. Turing is now considered one of the most influential theorists of early computer development and computer science and is also referred to as the *founding father of AI*. His book "Can a Machine Think?" from 1950 is a pioneering work in AI. (Turing, 1950) The *Turing Test* named after him examines whether a machine demonstrates human-like intelligence. In this test, a human evaluator communicates in writing with two interlocutors—one human and one AI—without knowing which is which. If the evaluator cannot reliably distinguish the AI from the human, the AI has passed the test and is considered "intelligent." The key question is whether the AI can convincingly imitate human thought processes. The Turing Test forms an important foundation for the field of artificial intelligence.

Turing Test with ChatGPT. Cameron R. Jones and Benjamin K. Bergen investigated at the beginning of 2024 whether ChatGPT 4 already passes the Turing Test. They conducted a public online test with a large number of participants. They implemented the "Imitation Game" described by Turing as a kind of chat exchange between people and various AI language models and compared the results. Participants and AIs were randomly assigned as questioner ("interrogator") or respondent ("witness"). The game involved 402 participants who communicated in a total of 1,979 rounds ("games") with one of 45 bots prepared by prompt, based on the GPT-3.5 and GPT-4 models. ChatGPT-4 performed best of all models. In 49.7% of cases, GPT-4 was classified as human. However, this result was surpassed when a real human responded—then, in 66% of cases, the questioners assumed they were communicating with a human. (Jones & Bergen, 2024) In a subsequent study, the prompts were optimized. This time, 402 participants took part in the game and communicated in a total of 1,979 rounds. In 54% of cases, GPT-4 was classified as human. When a real human responded, the questioners assumed they were communicating with a human in 67% of cases. (online, 2024), (Jones & Bergen, People cannot distinguish GPT-4 from a human in a Turing test, 2024).

Turing Test and *Interacting Agent*. The Turing Tests have been further developed to assess the capabilities of AI systems in realistic scenarios. One example is the study "Can Machines Imitate Humans? Integrative Turing Tests for Vision and Language Demonstrate a Narrowing Gap" by Golan et al. (2022). This research examines how well AI agents can imitate human behavior in various tasks by testing both visual and linguistic abilities.

Further Developments Since the 1950s

Compared to the early days of AI in the 1950s, language models and their combination with robotics have advanced significantly, making it sensible to adapt the Turing Test to modern environments and systems.

The Interacting Agent is thus a modern approach to evaluating the capabilities of artificial intelligence (AI). It is often seen as an evolution or adaptation of the classic Turing Test, originally developed by Alan Turing to determine whether a machine can simulate human-like thinking. The Interacting Agent aims to evaluate AI in more realistic and dynamic scenarios.

Core Idea of the Interacting Agent. An Interacting Agent is an AI that not only provides static answers to questions but is also capable of acting, learning, and handling complex tasks in interactive environments. Its abilities are assessed based on its interactions with humans and/or other agents.

Examples

Embodied AI Challenges: Here, AI agents interact in simulated environments (e.g., a virtual kitchen) and must perform tasks such as cooking a recipe. The evaluation focuses on how well they perceive, plan, and act within the environment.

Multi-Agent Systems: In tests involving multiple agents, they must collaboratively solve tasks and problems, such as coordinating resources within a team or developing competitive strategies.

Video Games as Test Environments: Games like Minecraft or StarCraft serve as platforms to test Interacting Agents in strategic and creative scenarios.

The focus here is particularly on the Interacting Agent demonstrating special abilities such as perception (via sensors), planning (strategies for achieving goals), action (executing actions), learning, communication, and teamwork. (Zhang, 2024).

Recent Developments

The most recent practical developments in AI can be followed in the media; for example, AI successes in quiz shows like Jeopardy (2011), victories against the world's best players in board games such as chess (1997) or Go (2016), self-driving cars (beginning in 1968), or chatbots like ChatGPT (2019)—to name just a few. The annual IJCAI conferences (International Joint Conferences on AI) provide overviews of the most important scientific findings in AI. Recently, AI research has been heavily funded by governments.

The Term "Artificial Intelligence"

John McCarthy (9/4/1927–10/23/2011) was an American logician, computer scientist, and author.

In his 1955 funding proposal to the Rockefeller Foundation for the Dartmouth Conference in the summer of 1956, McCarthy coined the term "Artificial Intelligence" as "the science and engineering of making intelligent machines, especially intelligent computer programs. It is related to the similar task of using computers to understand human intelligence, but AI does not have to confine itself to methods that are biologically observable." ("AI is the science and engineering of developing intelligent machines, especially intelligent computer programs.") (McCarthy, 2004), (McCarthy, Personal homepage of John McCarthy with references and cross-references to interesting publications and contributions, 2001).

John McCarthy is also the inventor of the programming language LISP.

1.4 Moore's Law: Computing Power Drives AI

AI has has been around since the 1950s. After an initial boom until the mid-1980s, investments in AI models and algorithms declined significantly as personal computers made their way into companies and almost every household. It is only in the last few years that AI has regained widespread interest, as computing power—which doubles roughly every 10 to 14 months according to Moore's Law—now

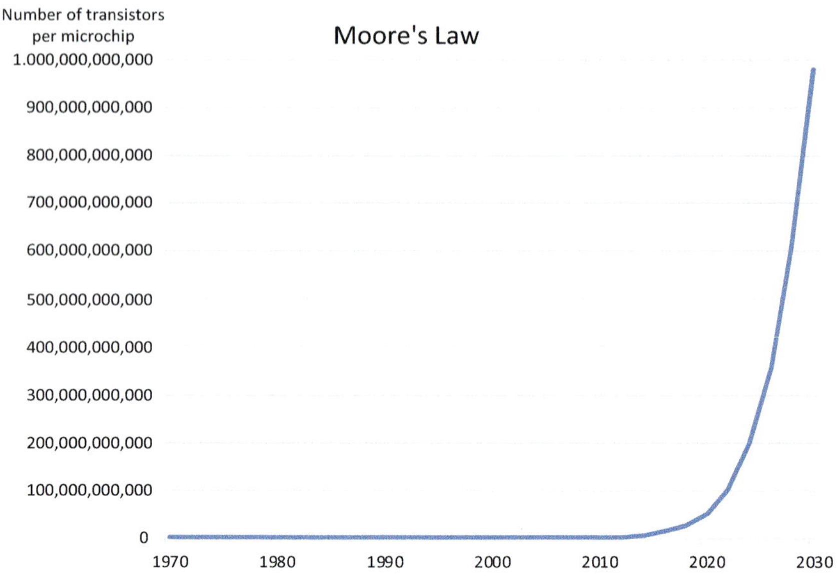

Fig. 1.4 Moore's Law

provides the capacity to analyze big data in real time (Fig. 1.4). Language models like ChatGPT have been around for decades, but they were mainly used internally by individual companies for process workflows, early warning systems, and predictive analytics.

1.5 Overview of Use Cases

Gaming: Decision trees, as used by chess computers. Here, the so-called calculation depth is crucial. The more powerful the computer, the better it performs.

Machine Learning: Evolving decision trees that, through new knowledge, also change previous paths. In healthcare, for example, AI is used for diagnostic procedures, personalized medicine, and to assist in surgeries.

Autonomous Driving: Self-driving cars use AI to understand their environment and navigate safely, as well as to "communicate" with other cars and objects (such as traffic lights, road signs). In addition, AI will control passenger comfort—ranging from favorite music, reading the daily news aloud, displaying videos, playing podcasts, or providing entertainment with jokes and quizzes.

AI algorithms are used, for example, in financial technology to develop investment strategies (example: robo-advisors), detect fraud, and optimize customer service.

Speech and Image Recognition: AI-powered technologies enable efficient and accurate recognition or analysis, from chatbots and virtual assistants to advanced security systems.

Videos featuring an AI avatar, for example, allow a company to automatically create explainer videos for customers, employees, and trainees based on existing internal documentation and with the support of a language model like ChatGPT.

In social media, however, increased vigilance is required, as this technology also enables the spread of deceptively realistic fake news. The AI can even move the avatar's lips to match almost any language. The translation is also performed automatically.

Automation is the key to enormous efficiency. Almost all digital processes can be automated with the help of AI. AI can already answer simple email inquiries, such as questions about opening hours or directions.

Cobots: In industry, collaborative robots (cobots) are increasingly being equipped with AI, enabling more effective and safer collaboration with humans. They perform multiple tasks and can also detect and avoid obstacles—for example, the people they work with ... a little fun fact ☺.

Robotics: Robots assist in assembly and are used in elderly care to relieve caregivers (keyword: strength support through AI-powered exoskeletons) and to improve the quality of life for older people. We will also see these helpers more frequently in construction and in households.

Environmental Protection: AI could play a decisive role in monitoring and combating environmental changes and in developing sustainable technologies.

Internet of Things—in English, *Internet of Things (IoT)*: By networking many systems with sensors, especially in logistics, ranging from roads, cars, and buses to charging stations, rest areas, containers, trucks, ships, and much more. The possibilities are limitless. And almost everyone already knows it on a small scale—as a smart home.

Security

At the AI Safety Summit in *Bletchley*, UK, in early November 2023, experts from around the world met to debate global security measures. Representatives from 28 countries, including the USA, China, the UK, EU members, and leading tech companies, agreed to address the potential risks of AI models like ChatGPT. The initial focus is on the largest, most powerful AI systems, as these currently have the potential to spread dangers, such as fake news or instructions for building bombs, etc.

The EU subsequently introduced the *AI Act* on August 1, 2024, which regulates safety. The AI Act will be tightened in phases.

Bletchley Park, about 70 km northwest of London, was once the headquarters of the British codebreaking service (Government Code and Cypher School) during World War II. Alan Turing and his team decrypted the *Enigma code* (the German Wehrmacht's radio encryption) here. Decoding the code was a decisive factor in the Allies' victory in the submarine Battle of the Atlantic and the North African campaign. The Enigma code was actually considered unbreakable.

2
AI Organization in the Company

Contents

Most companies in Germany and Europe still do not seem to have recognized the added value and benefits of AI for their business. Only 20% of companies in Germany are already using AI. This places Germany above the EU average, but it is not among the leading countries in Europe, ranking only seventh.

According to the Federal Statistical Office, in 2024 one in five companies (20%) in Germany used artificial intelligence (AI) technologies. This represents an 8% increase compared to 2023 (12%) and a 9% increase since 2021 (11%). The statistics include legal entities with at least ten employees. (Federal Statistical Office, 2024)

H. Knödel and D. Seipel, *AI and Bots in Everyday Life*,
https://doi.org/10.1007/978-3-658-51144-9_2

This chapter illustrates that AI is not just an abstract theory, but a practical tool with immediate impact. Vivid examples demonstrate how AI influences our daily lives. From the smartphone in our pocket to autonomous driving—AI is everywhere.

2.1 AI as a Top Management Priority

From our perspective, artificial intelligence is not just hype, but a strategic key factor that will be crucial for a company's competitiveness. It requires courage, vision, and a willingness to embrace new things. Those who act today will have a competitive advantage tomorrow—and this is vital for our small and medium-sized businesses (SMEs). AI is a top management issue because it has the potential to secure the future of our company. That is why it is so important to engage with basic AI knowledge as early as possible, to inform employees about the opportunities and risks of AI, and to analyze and identify ways in which AI can create added value and progress within the company. On the other hand, a company's entry into AI should be well thought out and closely aligned with the company's vision and strategy.

2.1.1 Vision and Outlook

AI is not a passing trend, but a tool that makes our processes more efficient, our products smarter, and our customer service more personalized. At the same time, people should remain at the center—and use AI as support. It is especially valuable when a company succeeds in maintaining its culture and values even as it integrates AI.

2.1.2 Strategy Development

Are you wondering how to develop a strategy that fits your business goals and enables the smoothest possible transition from the current productive world to a smart world with AI, without your company losing productivity, efficiency, and impact, but instead optimally enhancing value creation?

An effective strategic approach that we like to use in workshops is the *Disney Creative Strategy*. It allows you to dream imaginatively, like Walt Disney once did, to plan the dream realistically, and to critically question it. Through several cycles, you come as close as possible to a realistic, actionable strategy that leaves plenty of room for growth and innovation. During this strategy process, several employees are involved and can contribute their experience, knowledge, and innovative ideas. However, many apply the Disney Method incorrectly by neglecting or underestimating the framework conditions of time and space, thus finding a quick solution for their strategy, but one that cannot be implemented sustainably.

That is why we recommend being guided by an experienced strategy consultant when applying this approach.

2.1.3 Innovation Methods

Digitalization, the application of AI, and automation are creating many new, innovative opportunities. Some are immediately obvious. Others are not immediately recognizable or apparent. Here, it is worthwhile to dig a little deeper and use suitable methods to develop new innovative ideas.

Most German companies have at least heard of the Greenfield approach, field research, customer surveys, rapid prototyping, the principle of iteration, and similar methods. But according to our author Heiko's experience, only about 10 to 20% can really make use of the *Design Thinking* method, whereas in the USA, for example, it is nearly 100%. This is partly because Design Thinking is already taught at college level in the USA. In Germany, apart from modern technology startups and innovation departments of large corporations, Design Thinking is more or less seen as a meaningless buzzword. Here, *Design* is reduced to product layout, architectural design, or the description of a product's form.

Stanford University developed Design Thinking in the early 1990s, and the Hasso Plattner Institute brought Design Thinking to Europe in the early 2000s. Our author Heiko can proudly claim to have been a business coach for one of the first Design Thinking projects in Germany in 2009. Since then, the topic has fascinated him. He says: "I believe Bauhaus, Aldi, Lidl, and Bosch have intuitively applied it in many areas from the very beginning. But when I talk to employees and managers from German SMEs, 9 out of 10 conversation partners have never heard of it or only know it superficially. In German, Design Thinking is mainly associated with architecture and design."

We would like to point out that the term *Design* in American English encompasses much more than the German term *Design*. "*Design*" corresponds to the German word "*Gestaltung*", but hardly anyone here is aware of this. It is about "form, function, and design," as Steve Jobs explained during the development of the iPhone—and as an American boat builder reminded Heiko during a conversation over dinner while on vacation in Provence in 2022.

Design Thinking, in short, is a method for solving complex problems and developing innovative ideas.

2.1.4 The First Steps

A strategic approach begins with the question: Where can AI create added value? Where are there processes or areas in my company that I can automate or improve and make more efficient with the help of AI, compared to today? Instead of turning the entire company upside down, we identify areas that benefit most from *automation* and *data value creation*. This could be in production planning, customer service, inventory optimization, training, or marketing. A small success in a pilot project, a so-called *quick win*, gives us the confidence and knowledge to apply and roll out AI step by step.

2.1.5 Using Knowledge and Data as Fuel

AI is only as good as the people who use it. That is why we sensibly invest in the further training of our employees. *Seminars*, *workshops*, and *training sessions* ensure that the team learns what AI can do and where dangers and limitations lie. Employee acceptance increases when they can participate in the conversation, rather than being afraid of change.

A solid data foundation is essential. The majority of all company information and data is already digitized (if you still need to catch up here, you should seriously worry about your future). Now we review our data landscape and prepare it for AI applications. In doing so, we consider not only technical requirements, but also data protection, ethical guidelines, and regulatory requirements, for example regarding the AI Act, NIS-2, or DORA. This is a particularly sensitive issue for SMEs.

2.1.6 Cooperation and Consulting

When it comes to employee training and development, it is also possible to join forces with like-minded companies. This way, you foster exchange from the very beginning, develop a community, advance yourself and your company through mutual inspiration, and save costs.

Collaboration with experts, startups, and universities is also helpful and beneficial for developing AI capabilities in a tailored and cost-efficient way. The German SME sector thrives on networks—and AI innovations should be no exception.

2.1.7 Adaptation and Scaling

AI implementation does not guarantee success. Here, too, the success of implemented solutions can be measured using clear KPIs. This creates the opportunity to identify potential for adaptation and further development and to optimize along the KPIs. Only when an AI project creates measurable added value do we scale it to other business areas or target groups.

2.2 AI for Executives

Fun fact: Some employees might wish their manager were replaced by a robot with AI. Some managers might wish that certain employees were replaced by AI. Joking aside, for executives, artificial intelligence can be much more than just a technical tool—it is a potential strategic sparring partner that helps make more informed decisions and understand complex interrelationships more quickly. To achieve this, it is important to use AI in a targeted way that clearly adds value to leadership work. AI for executives is not a replacement, but an enhancement. It enables us to lead more strategically, proactively, and humanely. However, this requires openness, a clear foundation of values, and a willingness to develop oneself further. Because in the end, the following holds true: Even the best AI is only as good as the mind that uses it.

2.2.1 Smart Early Warning Systems and Intelligent Data Management

As eexecutives, we juggle countless pieces of information every day: product sales, revenue, customer satisfaction, market developments, employee feedback, financial forecasts, and much more. AI helps to systematize and analyze large volumes of data and to recognize patterns that we might overlook with the naked eye. For example, AI can serve as an early warning system for market changes or support us in identifying risks. With the help of customer personas, marketing can be improved and customer service optimized. Products are developed to suit the target group and do not contain unnecessary frills. Employee sentiment can be better captured with sensors and AI, for example through honest analysis of tone and language patterns instead of feigned statements like “Everything is fine. I am very satisfied.” This does not make managers redundant—no, it makes them more efficient.

2.2.2 AI Tools for the Executive of Tomorrow

AI tools help to evaluate key figures, optimize and automate processes, simplify workflows, automate tests, improve quality, relieve employees, and create operational as well as financial decision templates or even make automated decisions.

Moreover, AI also has the potential, despite its technical algorithms, to bring us closer to the people we lead. Through intelligent analysis tools, we can better understand the needs of our employees and teams, recognize moods, and create individual development plans. We can address each employee's strengths more specifically. Emotional and empathetic leadership becomes easier with AI—this may sound paradoxical, but it is true. Employees adapt to their needs and change over time. Since our body cells renew themselves approximately every seven years, our character, behavior and perspectives may also change. This is not always clearly noticeable, but there is a reason for the statistically calculated "seven-year itch" in marriages and careers. As a manager of many employees, you face major challenges.

Heiko knows from mindset practice and experience as an executive coach that we cannot change people. Everyone can only change themselves. We can provide an impetus, show possibilities, highlight potential, and give hints—but change always comes from within, not from outside (except in cases of force). Therefore, we as executives must adapt our tactics and leadership style to lead successfully and ideally create a pull effect as role models. For managers who have difficulty controlling and reflecting on themselves, AI tools will provide wonderful support and help them become more successful.

These tools support the executive, build trust, strengthen relationships, and make us better decision-makers.

2.2.3 Efficient Planning

Who doesn't know it: strategy meetings that get lost in endless discussions? AI can help here by calculating scenarios, simulating opportunities and risks, and making suggestions for optimal resource planning.

This gives us more time for what really matters—setting the strategic direction and inspiring our team.

2.2.4 Fear of Losing Control?

Hardly any executive likes to give up control:

- Delegating tasks? – Yes, gladly.
- Transferring responsibility? – Yes, gladly.
- Giving up control? – No, absolutely not.

It is crucial to maintain control. AI provides suggestions, but we are still the ones making the decisions. The human remains the captain; AI is only the pilot. Leadership does not mean relying on algorithms, but seeing them as support that complements our human intuition. This is, among other things, a point that is explained in detail under the aspect of AI ethics (see Sect. 9.4).

There are situations in which AI will make a decision. This can be illustrated quite clearly using the example of *autonomous driving*. For instance, if a tree falls onto the road during a storm while driving, a decision must be made within a fraction of a second whether to initiate an emergency stop and accept a collision with the tree, or to swerve, which can have further serious consequences, such as endangering pedestrians, driving into a ditch, or similar. Especially when human lives are at risk, ethics come into play.

Simple decisions—such as sorting out finished products into the reject pile if they show corresponding quality defects—can already be carried out by algorithms or AI. When it comes to team decisions, the situation is somewhat different. (Grählert, 2022)

Our primary goal in making decisions involving people will be to use AI in such a way that it prepares decision-making processes, provides meaningful information for quick decisions, and possibly also makes a recommendation. However, the decision should still rest with the responsible individuals.

2.2.5 Leadership During Transformation

As executives, we must be role models in dealing with AI. We must reduce fears, create transparency, and show our employees how they can grow with AI. Those who preach digitalization must also live it—and that starts with us.

Every executive can strengthen their mindset for this. Visualizing situations or using storytelling are also effective ways to successfully implement AI in the company. One of our favorite analogies for introducing AI is the computerization of the 1990s. With the development of personal computers in the late 1980s, applications were quickly developed that made writing letters, calculating in forms and spreadsheets, and structuring and using data in databases much easier. There were many very good applications, the best known being the Microsoft Office products, which made PCs acceptable in the workplace and rendered typewriters, accounting ledgers, paper-based calculations, and much more obsolete. Today, we write emails instead of letters, use MS Excel for all sorts of things, use accounting software instead of T-accounts, present with MS PowerPoint instead of an overhead projector—and all of this has become second nature. Would you really like to turn back time and work again with overhead projectors and typewriters?—Probably not. So why are we looking so extremely pessimistically into the future regarding AI? The fear of losing control existed in the 1990s as well. The fear of job loss existed in the 1990s as well. And indeed, many old jobs disappeared. However, they were replaced by even more new jobs. Work today is overall more technical, and there are many new technical professions. And this development will continue. Which farmer in 1900 would have believed that by 2024 there would often be only one farmer in a village, sometimes even a large-scale agricultural operation spanning several villages, who, with IT- and AI-supported agricultural machinery costing more than half a million euros, and with only a few employees, would harvest more than hundreds of farmers did in 1900, all of whom invested a lot of sweat and effort in sowing and harvesting.

2.3 Establishing an AI Competence Center

Whenever a paradigm shift occurs or a new technology is introduced, it makes sense to build internal company knowledge and expertise. To ensure this process is structured and, above all, organized within the company, setting up a Competence Center is a suitable approach.

The advantages of a Competence Center (CC) are that it brings together employees from different departments with varying experiences and levels of knowledge, who, for example, dedicate part of their working time as an interdisciplinary team to the further development of AI within the company and serve as points of contact for colleagues. They do not need to work full-time in the CC; instead, depending on the needs and required speed of AI adoption, they can participate in workshops, projects, and training programs. Additionally, they contribute insights and perspectives from their respective departments, ensuring that the largest possible area of the company is involved in the introduction of AI and a holistic transition is guaranteed. At the same time, there is flexibility to introduce individual areas to AI earlier and to plan and implement cross-departmental pilot projects in joint coordination, or to set up a so-called sandbox as a testing ground.

Best Practice: Establish an Interdisciplinary AI Team

The idea of an AI Competence Center is more than just the introduction of a new technology. It represents a cultural shift, an innovation platform, and a strategic driver for the future viability of the company. Especially for medium-sized businesses, such a center offers the opportunity to establish artificial intelligence (AI) not only as a technical tool but as a core competency that is considered across departmental boundaries.

The Concept: Interdisciplinary Collaboration as the Key

The idea of an AI Competence Center is based on the conviction that collaborative intelligence is the key factor for sustainable innovation. Collaboration here involves the members of the interdisciplinary team, who exchange ideas, work together, and complement each other, and, by incorporating AI as a technology, lay the foundation for sustainable innovation. (IT Verlag für Informationstechnik GmbH, 2024)

The Heart of an AI Competence Center

The heart of an AI Competence Center is interdisciplinary teams composed of dedicated employees from various departments. They combine the expertise of their respective domains with enthusiasm for new technologies and are tasked with promoting AI within the company and actively supporting their colleagues. At the same time, they serve as a bridge between technological possibilities and business requirements.

Such a team typically consists of members from IT, production, marketing, sales, finance, and human resources. Each team member invests a defined portion of their working time in the further development of AI projects and is also available as a point of contact for colleagues. They take on different roles: some act as *AI ambassadors* and bring technological possibilities into their departments, while others serve as *project managers* steering cross-departmental initiatives. There are also *innovation mentors* who support their colleagues in identifying and purposefully implementing AI potential.

The First Phase: Building the Competence Center

The establishment of an AI Competence Center begins with a clear objective: AI is to be anchored as a driver for efficiency, innovation, and competitiveness within the company (Harbort, 2024). Implementation takes place in several steps, starting with a detailed *needs analysis* to identify the areas where AI offers the greatest added value. Suitable employees are then selected who possess both technical understanding and a passion for innovation and communication skills, and who will serve as the first *members of the team*.

This is followed by comprehensive *training*, in which the team is familiarized with the fundamentals of AI, change management, and relevant tools, so that they can later act as multipliers within the company. Finally, an initial cross-departmental *pilot project* is carried out, serving as a showcase to build trust and acceptance for AI initiatives within the company.

The Second Phase: Scaling and Embedding

Once the AI Competence Center is established, the focus shifts to scaling successes and further increasing acceptance. Employees need a *point of contact* for their questions and concerns regarding AI. The AI Competence Center team acts as a "helpdesk" for AI-related questions and offers workshops and training sessions.

Internal communication is also important. Regular updates and success stories promote transparency and motivation. Through open and transparent communication with the entire workforce, the role of AI can be highlighted within the context of the company's vision, mission, and strategy. Furthermore, all employees are informed about progress and successes related to AI. Communication also serves to warn about risks, cyberattacks, and more.

The use of *feedback loops* provides additional value. This allows employees to contribute their ideas and either participate as part of an extended circle or act as idea generators and advisors. The progress of the AI Competence Center is regularly evaluated, and new needs and insights from the workforce are incorporated into the work and reflected upon through feedback loops.

The Role of the Consultant for Guidance and Clarity

By bringing in a consultant, the team can be supplemented with additional know-how, expertise, and experience in the AI field. The consultant can take on various roles: acting as an architect for the vision and strategy of the AI Competence Center and, at the same time, as a companion who provides the company with security during the change process. In addition, the consultant offers assistance, support, and training in the area of technological know-how.

Their tasks can focus on various priorities. In *strategic planning*, the consultant ensures that the orientation of the AI Competence Center is closely linked to the company's goals, so that AI initiatives are not isolated but are considered an integral part of the business strategy. As a *mentor*, the consultant supports team members in their role as AI ambassadors, helps them further develop their skills, and provides them with tools to disseminate their knowledge within the company. In the area of *change management*, the consultant guides the transformation process by identifying resistance, developing solutions, and taking measures to reduce reservations and create company-wide acceptance for AI. The consultant specifically employs communication strategies and practical approaches to inspire employees about the potential of AI. Furthermore, the consultant is responsible for building technological expertise by conducting specific AI training sessions, offering hands-on training, and promoting *knowledge transfer* within the company. In this way, the consultant makes a significant contribution to ensuring that the AI Competence Center can operate successfully in the long term.

Conclusion: From an Idea to the Company's DNA
An AI Competence Center is not a project with an end date, but a continuously evolving platform. It not only strengthens the company's technological expertise but also fosters a culture of learning, experimentation, and collaboration. With interdisciplinary teams as the driving force, AI becomes an integral part of the company's DNA, preparing medium-sized businesses for the challenges of the future. (Blocher, 2025)

2.4 Establishing AI Governance

Similar to IT governance, AI governance is strongly recommended in order to define and control uniform standards and rules for handling AI. Governance is also crucial for monitoring and complying with regulatory requirements, considering and implementing aspects of the EU Commission's AI Act, and protecting the company from external threats such as cyberattacks. *AI governance* encompasses the strategies, structures, processes, and policies that govern the use of artificial intelligence (AI) in a company. The goal is to ensure that AI is used in a way that is safe, ethical, transparent, and efficient. At the same time, *compliance* with legal and regulatory requirements must be ensured.

AI governance is essential to ensure the responsible and efficient use of artificial intelligence within a company. A central aspect is the fulfillment of *regulatory requirements*, as laws such as the European Union's AI Act set clear rules for dealing with AI. Without structured governance, it becomes difficult to comply with these requirements and avoid legal risks. At the same time, solid governance contributes to *risk minimization*, since the use of AI also brings challenges. These include risks such as incorrect decisions, ethical issues, or security vulnerabilities, which can be identified, controlled, and minimized through a clear strategy.

Moreover, well-designed AI governance has a significant impact on a company's *reputation*. Organizations that handle AI transparently and responsibly gain the trust of customers, employees, and business partners. This not only strengthens the brand but also increases the acceptance of new technologies within the company. Another key advantage lies in the *efficiency and innovative capacity* that structured AI governance promotes. Instead of individual AI projects running uncoordinated and in isolation, unified management ensures strategic alignment, better resource utilization, and more sustainable added value. In this way, AI is not only used safely and in compliance with regulations, but also purposefully leveraged to enhance competitiveness.

How do I set up AI governance analogous to IT governance?

Uniform standards and rules are important from the outset for the use and development of AI. If every employee does as they please and can use any AI tools, chaos ensues and synergy effects are completely lost. Furthermore, this increases the risk that confidential information leaks outside the company and circulates externally.

Minimizing risks that can arise from the use of AI (e.g., data protection violations, discriminatory algorithms) is one of the most important goals in AI governance.

It is also advisable to integrate the AI strategy into the corporate strategy and to *support the company's strategic goals*. If AI objectives run counter to the company's existing business goals, this can have devastating consequences for the company and its existence.

What are the central components of AI governance?

AI governance consists of several key components that ensure artificial intelligence is used responsibly, efficiently, and with strategic alignment within the company. An essential element is the **strategy**, which defines what *role AI* should play within the organization—whether as a driver of innovation or for process automation. This strategy must be closely aligned with the overarching *corporate strategy* to optimally integrate long-term goals and economic benefits.

Another important building block is **rules and policies** that set the ethical and legal framework for the use of AI. *Ethics guidelines* help to avoid bias and discrimination in AI systems and establish clear requirements for responsible use. *Transparency requirements* ensure that AI decisions are traceable and that their use is documented. In addition, *data protection* plays a central role by ensuring that all AI applications comply with the requirements of the *GDPR (General Data Protection Regulation)* and other data protection laws.

Risk management is a crucial component of AI governance, as the use of AI also entails *risks*. These include security vulnerabilities, faulty algorithms, or incorrect decisions, which can have serious consequences. Therefore, risks must be regularly assessed, monitored, and minimized through targeted measures.

Clear responsibilities are equally important. It must be clearly defined who in the company is *responsible* for handling AI. This includes *roles* such as data scientists, AI compliance officers, or executives involved in decision-making processes. A central *AI governance board* can be established to ensure that policies are followed and measures are consistently implemented.

Sustainable management also requires an effective **monitoring and control system.** *Performance monitoring* ensures that AI systems deliver the desired results, while *compliance checks* make sure that all applications comply with internal and external regulations. In addition, regular *audits* are necessary to review AI models for security, fairness, and accuracy and to make adjustments as needed.

Another crucial factor is **training and awareness** for employees. AI can only be used effectively and responsibly if all stakeholders understand its opportunities and risks. *Continuing education* and *training* help to impart knowledge about AI, recognize ethical challenges, and integrate *best practices* into daily work routines.

Finally, **technological standards** play a central role in AI governance. Clear requirements for *data quality*, *model training*, and *security requirements* must be defined to ensure high reliability and efficiency of AI systems. Through *benchmarking* and adherence to best practices, the company can ensure that its AI development and use are always state-of-the-art.

With comprehensive AI governance, it can be ensured that AI is not only technologically powerful, but also ethically acceptable, secure, and economically viable when integrated into the company.

Example implementation of AI governance

As a first step, an AI governance board should be established, composed of representatives from IT, compliance, legal, data protection, and operational departments. This board can monitor the processes, implementations, prototypes, and *progress of AI projects.* It also supports strategy development by creating an AI strategy that is compatible with the corporate strategy. Furthermore, it is responsible for planning and approving new AI projects.

Subsequently, it is advisable to define *guidelines* for AI use. These contain important rules and requirements that are adapted to the company's values and ethics. Examples include statements such as "*AI systems may only be trained on verified and non-discriminatory datasets.*" or "*All decisions made by AI systems must be transparently documented.*".

A *risk-based approach* is also important. High-risk AI applications (e.g., in human resources or safety-critical areas) are subject to stricter controls and must undergo regular audit checks. (IEEE (Institute of Electrical and Electronics Engineers), 2024)

In addition, *transparency measures* should be implemented to disclose to employees and customers where and how AI is used. AI-generated content should be clearly labeled.

Comparison: AI Governance vs. IT Governance

(See Table 2.1)

AI Governance and the European Union AI Act

The *AI Act* of the European Union sets out specific requirements that demand a sensitive approach to AI tools and AI-generated information—both as sender and receiver. These requirements are aimed at ensuring the safe, transparent, and ethical use of AI systems. The most

Table 2.1 AI Governance vs. IT Governance

Aspect	IT Governance	AI Governance
Focus	IT systems and infrastructure	AI systems, algorithms, and data
Objectives	Efficiency, cost control, security	Ethics, fairness, transparency, legal compliance
Regulation	Data protection, IT security laws	Data protection, AI-specific laws (e.g., AI Act)
Monitoring	Monitoring of IT performance	Control of AI outcomes and their impacts

efficient way to comply with these guidelines is to establish *AI governance* within the organization. (Future of Life Institute, 2024)

Key Aspects of the AI Act

The AI Act classifies AI systems according to their risk potential into categories such as *unacceptable risk*, *high risk*, and *low risk*. For high-risk systems, strict requirements are imposed that necessitate a robust governance structure. (Cornell University, 2024)

Requirements for High-Risk AI Systems

High-risk AI systems are subject to stringent requirements to ensure their safety, fairness, and transparency. A central aspect is *risk management*, which encompasses processes for identifying, assessing, and mitigating risks throughout the entire lifecycle of an AI system. Through continuous analysis and preventive measures, potential hazards are to be identified and minimized at an early stage.

Another important point is the *data and data quality requirements*. It must be ensured that the datasets used are free from bias and are of high quality. Faulty or unbalanced data can lead to discriminatory or erroneous decisions, making the review and cleansing of data essential.

Transparency is another key requirement, ensured through *detailed documentation and logging*. Companies must keep precise records of the design, development, and performance of their AI systems. This enables better traceability and facilitates the review of systems by regulatory authorities.

There is also a *transparency and information obligation* to ensure that users are clearly informed about how the AI system works and its decision-making processes. This builds trust and ensures that users are able to better understand and, if necessary, question the decisions made by an AI system.

A particularly important component is *human oversight*, i.e., human supervision of AI systems. According to the AI Act, this overarching control is especially required for high-risk AI systems (including, for example, medical procedures, as well as credit approval and applicant selection), so that humans can intervene in the AI system if necessary and shut it down if required. In addition, there is the component of *human in the loop* (i.e., human in the loop), which defines the approach when humans always make the decisions actively, while the AI system only provides suggestions and decision support. Companies must therefore establish mechanisms that enable humans to intervene in and control the decisions of the AI system. This is intended to prevent automated processes from making critical decisions without sufficient oversight, especially in safety-relevant or ethically sensitive areas.

Conformity Assessment and Market Surveillance

To ensure that high-risk AI systems meet all prescribed requirements, providers must carry out appropriate *conformity assessments*. These procedures serve to confirm compliance with the established regulations and to ensure that AI systems are operated in accordance with applicable regulations.

In parallel, national authorities are responsible for *market surveillance* and monitor whether companies comply with legal requirements. If violations are identified, appropriate measures can be taken to enforce compliance and minimize risks for consumers and businesses.

Establishment of Governance Structures

To provide overarching control of AI regulations, an *AI Office* will be established at the EU level. This central institution coordinates the implementation of the *AI Act*, supports companies in complying with the regulations, and oversees regulatory measures in the member states.

In addition, individual member states are required to designate *national competent authorities* responsible for the application and enforcement of AI regulations at the national level. These authorities are to support companies, monitor regulatory standards, and take enforcement action if necessary.

Through these comprehensive requirements and structured governance mechanisms, it is intended to ensure that high-risk AI systems are operated safely, fairly, transparently, and in compliance with the law, while at the same time fostering innovation and minimizing risks.

3

Large Language Models (LLMs) for Generative AI

Contents

Large language models, also known as LLMs, have fundamentally transformed how machines understand and use human language. These models, trained on vast and diverse datasets, are capable of generating text, translating, and even analyzing complex relationships. With their impressive ability to process natural language, they have found applications in nearly all areas of daily life, from personalized chatbots to creative text production. Their strength lies in the combination of language understanding and contextual analysis, enabling them to deliver increasingly precise and human-like responses. However, their growing capabilities also bring challenges, particularly in the areas of ethics, data privacy, and responsibility. Language models not only mark a technological milestone but also raise fundamental questions about the future of human-machine

H. Knödel and D. Seipel, *AI and Bots in Everyday Life*,
https://doi.org/10.1007/978-3-658-51144-9_3

interaction. In this chapter, we will discuss the language models of the largest providers and take a closer look at how they work, their areas of application, and the associated opportunities and risks.

3.1 Overview of Major Language Models

Large Language Models (LLMs) like ChatGPT made AI mainstream from the end of 2022, meaning that AI suddenly became accessible and usable for the general public.

With minimal effort and a few practical techniques, language models are a great asset in everyday writing and document editing, as well as when using best practice content, especially in programming. To access the language model of your choice, the easiest way is to search for the name of the model and then click on the corresponding link. Almost all language models are available for free to some extent; however, with most of them you still need to register with an email address and a password.

To use a language model, you can simply provide a rough idea to the model, assign it a specific role, and let it generate creative solutions for your idea. Suppose you want to write a romantic poem for your beloved. Romantic, for you, means it should be in the style of William Shakespeare. You can have this realized in no time and with little effort. Or you want a funny poem in the style of Erich Kästner, a limerick, or a fairy tale about yourself in the manner of the Brothers Grimm (our insider tip, because with such a fairy tale you can playfully find out what the internet knows about you—provided your name is not too common and you are not, by chance, named John Doe (the English equivalent of Max Mustermann).

There are countless useful applications, such as summarizing documents, creating social media content and strategies, preparing presentations, visualizing through creative images, translating a program flowchart (PAP) into any programming language, providing assistance and examples for programming, analyzing a document or answering targeted questions about its content (such as notice periods in a 30-page contract), analyzing a website, analyzing images, creating your own poems and fairy tales, using AI agents to plan and automatically execute tasks, and much more.

3.1.1 ChatGPT by OpenAI

Website: https://chat.openai.com

ChatGPT is a versatile AI tool that delivers exceptional performance in many areas. ChatGPT belongs to the field of generative AI, meaning it is best suited for text-based queries and communication tasks. It can also be used to automate tasks, increase productivity, and create high-quality content. Thanks to its ability to understand and generate natural language, it is particularly useful for creating and editing texts, supporting technical tasks, providing learning aids, and personalizing recommendations. (OpenAI, 2022).

Text Generation and Editing

ChatGPT can generate high-quality, coherent, and creative texts that can be used in various contexts with different perspectives and goals. Some *application examples* include:

- *Content creation:* Writing content such as blog articles, social media posts, and marketing materials.
- *Creative writing:* Creating stories, poems, and scripts.
- *Document editing:* Improving and correcting texts, creating summaries, and translations.

Conversational Abilities

ChatGPT can conduct natural and meaningful conversations, making it ideal for use in chatbots and customer service applications—and more recently, in the field of robotics. *Application examples* include:

- *Customer service:* Automated responses to customer inquiries and real-time problem solving.
- *Virtual assistants:* Support with daily tasks such as scheduling, reminders, and research on various topics.
- *Robots:* Through API interfaces to language models like ChatGPT, robots gain very natural language capabilities and, in addition to their original purpose, can become encyclopedias of world knowledge, able to answer a wide range of questions, be a good conversational partner, or translate languages.

Programming and Technical Support

ChatGPT can generate, debug, and explain programming code, making it a useful tool for developers. In particular, the new version *GPT-4o with canvas* is especially helpful for software developers, as code can be interpreted and improved in real time—even line by line. *Application examples* include:

- *Code generation:* Quickly creating code snippets for various programming languages.
- *Debugging:* Identifying and fixing errors in code, providing solutions, and serving as a basis for discussion.
- *Explanation of concepts:* Assisting in explaining complex technical concepts and algorithms.

Education and Learning Support

ChatGPT can create learning materials and explain complicated topics in an understandable way. *Application examples* include:

- *Homework help:* Support in solving assignments and explaining topics for pupils and students.
- *Creation of teaching materials:* Generating exercises, summaries, and learning aids for teachers and students.

Personalized Recommendations

ChatGPT can provide personalized recommendations based on user input, whether for books, movies, or other products. *Application examples* include:

- *Product advice:* Suggestions for suitable products or services based on the user's preferences and needs.
- *Content suggestions:* Recommending books, movies, or music based on the user's taste.

History

In November 2022, OpenAI launched ChatGPT as the first language model that was freely accessible to everyone. This marked the beginning of a new AI wave of AI adoption. Microsoft supported OpenAI with more than 10 billion US dollars and its infrastructure, and developed Bing Chat for its search engine, which is built on OpenAI's GPT models. Bing Chat was further developed into MS Copilot. ChatGPT and MS Copilot have established themselves as leading tools for various text- and image-related applications, which is why we highlight them separately here. *GPT* stands for "Generative Pre-trained Transformer" and refers to OpenAI's language models.

Available Models

The model *GPT-4o* was released in May 2024. It is suitable for simple research and all kinds of text processing. DALL-E is used for image generation. The model *GPT-4o mini* is suitable for general daily questions with fast response times.

At the end of February 2025, OpenAI released GPT-4.5. This model offers improved writing capabilities, expanded world knowledge, and more natural interaction capabilities. However, it does not introduce significantly new features and, in some areas, does not surpass specialized models such as o1 or o3-mini.

According to OpenAI CEO Sam Altman, the release of GPT-5 is planned for August or September 2025. This model will integrate significant technological advances, including the o3 reasoning model, and will combine various OpenAI technologies into one system to move closer to achieving artificial general intelligence (AGI). OpenAI is also working to design language models like GPT-5 so that they not only understand text, but can also plan actions, interpret environments, and control physical tasks. This also includes processing sensor and multimodal data (such as camera, microphone, motion sensors). This makes them even better suited for use in robots and creates a natural connection between thinking by AI and acting through robotics. Similarly, the topic of automation by AI agents is being advanced by the *MCP (Model Context Protocol)*, which was developed by Anthropic and released as open-source (open standard) in November 2024, so that in the future you will be able to perform file operations, email actions, scheduling, etc. directly and securely from within ChatGPT.

The model *GPT-4o with canvas* enables dialogue with ChatGPT in two side-by-side windows. On the right, we see the current results; on the left, the dialogue window. We can now enter our inputs as usual in the dialogue window and follow the results on the right. However, we can also specifically highlight individual words or lines of the result and change only those. This method is *especially helpful for programmers* and for *image analysis*. By default, ChatGPT generates a completely new result for every change request. That is, the entire program code changes. But if I only want to change a command, an output text, or a section of the code, I can now do this specifically with GPT-4o with canvas. You can also make changes to the result yourself.

The model *GPT-o1* is optimal for solving complex problems and focuses on advanced reasoning capabilities. Unlike general-purpose models, this model is designed to apply scientific methods and findings in a targeted manner. The computation time and thus the response time increase, as information and relationships are processed. However, the results are more accurate. The model *GPT-o1 mini* is based on GPT-o1. However, it features so-called *fast reasoning*, meaning the results are delivered in no time. With this, you get much faster results than with the GPT-o1 preview model, but they are also less accurate. While GPT-4o was focused on fast response times, for example for a chatbot, the new versions from o1 onwards are, according to technical specifications, trained to form so-called "*chains of thought*" (*chain-of-thought, COT*). They are therefore somewhat slower, but significantly more accurate and can solve complex problems.

Building on this, *GPT-o3* represents a further development in reasoning performance, offering improved efficiency and stronger results in complex problem-solving scenarios, and, for example, generates finished program code in seconds. Fun fact: Version 2 was skipped for trademark reasons (think of a British telecommunications company). In parallel, developments such as the Model Context Protocol (MCP) aim to enable language models to interact more directly with external systems, allowing secure execution of tasks such as file operations, scheduling, and communication workflows.

Versions

Under the version *ChatGPT Plus*, all ChatGPT versions available in the paid version are grouped together. Currently, a single license costs $20 per month for individual users, or $25 per month per user if you want to use the same environment as a team, for all kinds of complex questions with guaranteed, fast response times. The license can be canceled monthly. So if you just want to try out the Plus version or want to create your own AI agent with ChatGPT, which can be enhanced with additional information (such as multi-page prompts that can be uploaded via a separate PDF file), you can simply try it out for a month for $20 (currently about €20).

Since December 5, 2024, there is also the *ChatGPT Pro* version, which is primarily designed for companies and researchers with a high demand for AI resources. This costs $200 per month per license, offers unlimited access to all reasoning models and GPT-4o, extended access to Deep Research, access to the research preview of GPT-4.5, access to the o1 pro mode, which provides even more computing power for the best answers to the most difficult questions, and extended access to video generation with Sora.

3.1.2 Microsoft Copilot

Website: https://copilot.microsoft.com

Microsoft Copilot is an AI-powered tool integrated into the Microsoft 365 suite, developed to increase productivity and optimize workflows. MS Copilot is very helpful for *automating routine tasks*. Especially in combination with MS Power Automate, recurring tasks can be automated, saving a lot of time and increasing efficiency. (Microsoft, 2023).

Content Creation

Copilot can generate various types of content, from simple texts to complex documents.

Application examples:

- *Reports and presentations:* Automatically creating and formatting reports and PowerPoint presentations based on inputs and data.

- *Text suggestions:* Providing suggestions for emails, documents, and other written communication.
- *Email management:* Automatically sorting, filtering, and responding to emails.
- *Calendar management:* Scheduling and managing appointments and meetings.
- *Meeting minutes:* Transcribing MS Teams recordings
- *Excel tasks:* Creating formulas, executing calculations, and formatting in spreadsheets

Data Analysis and Visualization
Copilot can analyze data and transform it into comprehensible and useful visualizations.

Application examples:

- *Excel analyses:*Automatically creating charts, pivot tables, and other visualizations in Excel.
- *Data interpretation:* Providing insights and recommendations based on data analysis.

Meeting Assistance
Copilot can organize and support meetings by taking notes and assigning tasks.

Application examples:

- *Meeting minutes:* Automatically capturing meeting notes and to-do lists.
- *Agenda creation:* Preparing and distributing meeting agendas.

Integration with Other Microsoft 365 Applications
Copilot works seamlessly with other Microsoft 365 tools to create a unified and efficient work environment.

Application examples:

- *Teams integration:* Collaboration and communication within Microsoft Teams, including real-time suggestions and automated task distribution.

- *SharePoint and OneDrive:* Managing and organizing documents and files stored in SharePoint and OneDrive.

Microsoft Copilot is a versatile tool specifically designed to make daily work in companies easier and more productive. By automating routine tasks, supporting content creation and analysis, and integrating into the Microsoft 365 suite, Copilot helps optimize workflows and allows users to focus on more important tasks.

Thanks to its collaboration with OpenAI, Microsoft Copilot also uses a GPT-4 model and combines it with its own technologies. Microsoft has optimized the GPT-4 base model with its own algorithms and data to better tailor it to the Microsoft product range. Copilot's strength lies in its seamless integration into Microsoft products, enabling users to analyze and evaluate any context-related information from Office documents, emails, Teams videos, and more—however, this depends on the permissions and access rights within the company.

Those who purchase MS Copilot as part of Microsoft 365 can, with extensive permissions, process any data from MS Teams, MS Outlook, MS Excel, and MS Word, and, for example, have meeting minutes generated. In combination with Microsoft Power Automate (already included in the Microsoft 365 license), processes such as creating PowerPoint presentations, designing Excel spreadsheets, etc., can also be simplified and automated.

The license for MS Copilot as part of Microsoft 365 is subject to a fee (additional cost), but the browser version at the link above can also be used free of charge. However, registration or login is also required here.

3.1.3 LLaMA by Meta

Website: https://www.llama.com

LLaMA (Large Language Model Meta AI) is a powerful language AI developed by Meta,[1] specialized in understanding and generating

[1] Meta is the parent company of Facebook, Instagram, and WhatsApp.

human language. Below, we highlight some of LLaMA's key capabilities and how they can be utilized in various scenarios. (Meta, 2023)

Natural Language Processing (NLP)
LLaMA can analyze, understand, and generate text, making it ideal for a wide range of NLP tasks. *Example applications* include:

- *Text generation:* Creating blog posts, articles, and other written content based on input parameters.
- *Text summarization:* Reducing complex documents and texts to comprehensible summaries.
- *Translations:* Translating texts into different languages to facilitate communication.

Dialogue Systems and Chatbots
LLaMA can serve as the foundation for advanced chatbots that conduct natural and fluent conversations. *Example applications:*

- *Customer support:* Automating customer inquiries and providing instant responses.
- *Virtual assistants:* Assisting with daily tasks such as scheduling appointments and retrieving information.

Content Creation and Editing
LLaMA can create creative content and enhance existing texts. *Example applications:*

- *Creative writing:* Generating stories, poems, and scripts.
- *Proofreading:* Improving the grammar, spelling, and style of texts.

Personalized Recommendations
LLaMA can provide personalized recommendations based on user data and preferences. *Example applications:*

- *Product suggestions:* Recommendations for products or services based on user preferences.
- *Content suggestions:* Recommended books, movies, or music based on the user's taste.

Data Analysis and Interpretation
LLaMA can analyze large volumes of data and generate comprehensible insights. *Example applications:*

- *Market analysis:* Identifying trends and patterns in large datasets.
- *Automated reporting* and visualizations based on data analyses.

LLaMA is a versatile and powerful AI capable of handling a wide range of tasks in natural language processing, content creation, dialogue systems, and data analysis. As a result, LLaMA is well suited for companies seeking to increase their efficiency and productivity through the use of advanced language AI technology.

Model
The *LLaMA 3.1* model was released in April 2024 and is an open-source language model with 8 to 70 billion parameters. It offers improved reasoning and coding capabilities.

3.1.4 Gemini by Google (formerly Bard)

Website: https://gemini.google.com

Gemini is an advanced AI model from Google, specifically developed to support a wide range of tasks in natural language processing, multimodality, context-aware responses, translation, and data analysis. This makes Gemini particularly useful for businesses and freelancers looking to increase their efficiency and productivity through the use of advanced AI technology. (Google, 2023).

The development of Google's language models is a fascinating journey, so here we present a brief historical overview, ranging from LaMDA to Bard and up to the current Gemini version. Here is an overview of the key milestones:

In 2017, Google AI was founded, which developed LaMDA (Language Model for Dialogue Applications) in 2021. LaMDA is a neural network-based language model. It was specifically designed for dialogue applications and is distinguished by its ability to conduct human-like conversations. In 2022, LaMDA attracted attention when a Google engineer claimed the model had developed consciousness, sparking a broad debate about the ethics and potential of AI.

Bard was released in March 2023 as Google's response to ChatGPT and was Google's first attempt to make a conversational large language model (i.e., a chatbot) accessible to the general public. Originally, Bard was based on a lightweight version of LaMDA. Later, Bard was switched to PaLM 2 (Pathways Language Model 2), a more advanced language model that offered improved coding, multilingual, and reasoning capabilities. In February 2024, Bard was renamed Gemini. Gemini is Google's latest and most advanced AI model family, developed by Google DeepMind.

Model

Gemini is a multimodal model, which means it can process various types of information, including text, code, images, and more. Gemini exists in different product versions: **Gemini Nano** is an efficient model for mobile devices. **Gemini Pro** is a versatile model for a wide range of tasks. **Gemini Ultra** is the most powerful model for highly complex tasks. Gemini 1.5 Pro has a greatly expanded context window, enabling it to process very large amounts of information. Gemini is integrated into Google products such as Google Search, Ads, Chrome, and Duet AI for Google Workspace. (Google, Gemini – our largest and most powerful AI model, 2023), (Caramba by All-AI, 2025)

The use of Google Gemini is available free of charge, but there is also a paid Gemini Advanced version.

Natural Language Processing and Understanding (NLP)

Gemini can analyze, understand, and generate text. *Application examples:*

- *Text summarization:* Reducing complex texts to concise summaries.
- *Text generation:* Creating high-quality, coherent texts for various use cases, such as blog articles, technical documentation, and creative writing projects.
- *Understanding complex queries:* Thanks to the underlying LaMDA technology, finer nuances and long, complex inputs can be better understood, resulting in more precise and context-aware responses.

Multimodal Capabilities
Multimodal capabilities include *image description* and *video transcription*. Image description refers to generating text descriptions based on image content. Video transcription refers to the automatic creation of subtitles as well as summaries for video content.

Context-Aware Responses
Context-aware responses mean being able to conduct meaningful conversations with people that are grammatically and factually correct. This includes *dialogue systems*, which refers to the development of advanced chatbots capable of conducting fluent and context-aware conversations. *Virtual assistants*, in turn, support tasks that require deeper context processing, such as scheduling and personalized recommendations.

Translation Services
One area in which Google has been active for a long time is the translation of texts and *multilingual communication*. This refers to supporting the translation of documents, emails, and other texts to facilitate global communication. With the use of AI, translation tasks can be carried out more quickly and easily. In so-called *real-time translation*, translations are provided simultaneously for meetings and conversations.

Data Analysis and Interpretation
The main areas of application for data analysis and interpretation by AI are *business reports*. The creation of reports and analyses based on company data is largely fully automated.

AI applications like Gemini are also increasingly used for *market research*, for example in identifying trends and patterns in large datasets to make informed business decisions.

Integration into the Google Ecosystem
One advantage of Gemini is its seamless integration with *Google services:* Gemini is closely integrated with other Google products such as Google Search, Google Assistant, and Google Workspace. Another advantage is *real-time data access*. Gemini can access the internet in real time to provide up-to-date information.

Support for Programming
Compatibility with programming languages: Gemini supports over 20 programming languages and can generate and explain code.

Focus on Ethical and Responsible AI
Safety measures: Google has put safeguards in place to ensure that Gemini does not provide harmful or unreliable information.

3.1.5 Claude by Anthropic

Website: https://www.anthropic.com/claude or https://claude.ai

The company Anthropic was founded by former OpenAI researchers. *Claude* was developed by Anthropic and is based on the principle of '*Constitutional AI*' with *ethical and safety principles*. It offers robust safeguards against harmful content and places great emphasis on user-friendliness. Claude includes the widely known versions *Haiku*, *Sonnet*, and *Opus*. The following points highlight Claude's special capabilities. (Anthropic, 2023).

While other LLM models are optimized through manual *Reinforcement Learning*, Claude stands out for its focus on safety, ethical principles, and user-friendliness. With its "Constitutional AI" approach, it offers a novel methodology that makes it particularly suitable for safety-critical and ethical applications. Compared to models like ChatGPT,

Claude may be somewhat more conservative, but is therefore more robust and better suited for sensitive use cases. The Anthropic developers always keep innovation and safety in mind. They are pioneers in the field of automation through AI agents. Anthropic developed the MCP (Model Context Protocol) and released it as open-source (open standard) in November 2024. This allows actions such as file operations, email actions, scheduling, etc. to be performed directly from an LLM in a standardized and secure manner.

Focus on Safety and Ethical AI (Constitutional AI)
Claude is based on the principle of "Constitutional AI." This means the model was trained with a predefined "constitution" that includes ethical and safety principles. Claude's special features include:

- The model can justify its answers with moral considerations.
- It is designed to be particularly robust against harmful or abusive inputs.
- The goal is to reduce the likelihood that Claude generates toxic, misleading, or harmful content.

Strong Focus on User-Friendliness and Explainability
Claude is designed to interact especially well with users by providing clear and understandable answers. It aims to explain complex topics in simple terms, making it ideal for users without technical backgrounds. Compared to other LLMs, Claude places particular emphasis on clear explanations and "gentle" responses, whereas OpenAI's GPT models, for example, are known for their versatility.

Robustness Against "Prompt Injection" and Manipulation
Claude was designed to make it more difficult to manipulate the model or induce it to generate harmful or unauthorized content. Other models can, in certain scenarios, be tricked by clever inputs into providing harmful or undesirable content. Claude seeks to minimize such weaknesses through its security architecture.

Balanced Response Quality
Among Claude's *strengths* is its particular ability to conduct human-like conversations, often feeling "friendlier." It also delivers consistent and high-quality answers, especially for explanatory and argumentative tasks. Among Claude's *weaknesses* is that it may be less "creative" or "adventurous" than other LLMs when it comes to original or highly creative texts.

Faster Optimizations Through Smaller Iterations
Anthropic works iteratively on Claude and regularly releases improved versions based on user feedback and technical advances. The regular updates ensure a continuously improved user experience. In comparison, OpenAI releases new models less frequently, resulting in larger leaps between versions.

Openness to Long-Term Safety Research
Claude is the result of Anthropic's long-term vision to make AI safe and controllable. Limitations are deliberately built in. Claude strives to remain consciously safe and controllable, even if this sometimes leads to very conservative answers.

Specific Application Areas and Market Positioning
Claude is often used in areas where safety, explainability, and user-friendliness are paramount, such as education, medicine, or enterprise applications. While other LLMs are versatile and strong in creative and technical applications, Claude has been specifically optimized for safe and ethical use.

3.1.6 Mistral

Website: https://mistral.ai

Mistral is the LLM developed by the French AI startup Mistral AI, which has achieved remarkable progress with its language models, particularly *Mistral 7B*. Mistral 7B is a compact model with outstanding efficiency and open-source availability. Through efficient, powerful, and open language models, Mistral AI positions itself as a serious challenger in the field of large language models. The focus on efficiency, open-source development, and specialized capabilities—especially in programming—sets Mistral apart from other providers and offers companies flexible and customizable AI solutions. (Mistral AI, 2023)

Efficiency and Performance

- *Compact architecture:* Mistral 7B has 7.3 billion parameters and still outperforms larger models like LLaMA 2 with 13 billion parameters in benchmarks.
- *Innovative techniques:* By using Grouped-Query Attention (GQA) and Sliding Window Attention (SWA), Mistral 7B can process longer text sequences more efficiently while requiring fewer computational resources.

Open-Source Approach

- *Free availability:* Mistral AI has released its models, including Mistral 7B, under the Apache 2.0 license, enabling developers to review, adapt, and use the source code in their own projects.
- *Transparency and adaptability:* This open approach promotes transparency and allows companies to tailor the models to specific requirements without relying on proprietary solutions.

Specialization in Programming Code

Training on code data: Unlike many other language models, Mistral 7B was trained not only on natural language but also on programming code. This enables it to effectively perform tasks such as code completion and to outperform specialized models in certain areas.

Model

Agile development: Mistral AI has released several models in a short period, including Mistral 7B and Mistral 8×7B, and plans further releases. With this rapid iteration, Mistral AI aims to respond quickly to technological advances and market needs. The Mistral 8×7B model is an open-source model, although it still dates from the end of 2023.

Competitive Performance
Benchmark results: Mistral models have achieved impressive results in various tests and compete with established models such as GPT-4, particularly in areas like language understanding, mathematics, and programming.

European Origin and Funding
Strong growth: Mistral AI has received significant investments, including a funding round of 600 million euros, making the company a major player in the global AI market.

3.1.7 Neuroflash – made in Germany

Website: https://neuroflash.com

Neuroflash is a Germany-based company specializing in AI-powered text generation. It focuses on the German-speaking market with high-quality text creation and image generation, and is particularly well-suited for marketing and SEO while complying with European data protection standards. Compared to other large language models (LLMs), Neuroflash offers a tailored solution for companies seeking to create high-quality, targeted content in German. (neuroflash, 2021)

Specialization in the German-speaking Market
Optimized German text quality: Neuroflash was trained with the best German-speaking marketing experts and therefore delivers high-quality texts in German.

Integration of Text and Image Generation
All-in-one solution: In addition to text generation, Neuroflash also offers the ability to create AI-generated images, enabling comprehensive content creation within a single platform.

Personalization through "Personalities"
Individual text styles: The "Personalities" feature allows users to automatically adjust the style, tone, and address of generated texts to more effectively target specific audiences.

Focus on Marketing and SEO[2]
Specialized templates: Neuroflash offers over 20 different text types, including social media posts, advertising copy, and blog articles, specifically designed for marketing purposes.

SEO analysis: The platform includes tools for search engine optimization to increase the visibility of the created content.

Data Protection and Data Sovereignty
European data protection standards: As a company based in Germany, Neuroflash is subject to strict European data protection regulations, which can be a decisive advantage for many users.

User-Friendliness and Accessibility
Intuitive operation: The platform is designed to be easily accessible for both beginners and professionals, with flexible pricing models that also make it easier for small businesses and start-ups to access.

3.1.8 Aleph Alpha – the German Start-up Hope

Website: https://aleph-alpha.com/de

Aleph Alpha is a German AI company particularly suited for the public sector and safety-critical applications. With its Luminous models, Aleph Alpha offers a European AI solution characterized by multimodality, explainability, and a strong focus on data protection and the public sector. Compared to other large language models (LLMs), Aleph Alpha places special emphasis on transparency and compliance with European data protection standards. (Alpha, 2023)

[2] SEO = Search Engine Optimization.

European Data Sovereignty and Data Protection
Server location: Aleph Alpha operates its servers in Germany, ensuring full control over the data and compliance with the European General Data Protection Regulation (GDPR).

Multimodality
Text and image processing: Aleph Alpha's Luminous models are capable of processing and generating both text and images, enabling comprehensive analysis and content creation.

Explainability and Transparency
AtMan technology: Aleph Alpha has developed a method called AtMan that makes the AI's decision-making processes understandable, thereby making the models more trustworthy, especially in safety-critical areas.

Specialization in the Public Sector
Applications for administrations: Aleph Alpha offers AI solutions specifically tailored to the needs of public service, to optimize workflows and accelerate decision-making processes.

Integration of Fact-Checking
Trustworthy AI: By implementing fact-checking mechanisms in its models, Aleph Alpha aims to increase the accuracy and reliability of generated content.

European Alternative to US Providers
Independent development: Aleph Alpha positions itself as a European alternative to US AI providers, with the goal of strengthening technological sovereignty and data protection in Europe.

3.1.9 DeepSeek – the powerful challenger from China

Website: https://www.deepseek.com

DeepSeek is an advanced **large language model (LLM)** developed by the Chinese company **DeepSeek AI**, positioning itself as a serious competitor to Western AI models. With a combination of powerful algorithms, deep training on extensive datasets, and a clear focus on the Chinese market, DeepSeek is setting new standards for AI-generated language and text processing.

With the release of its R1 model, DeepSeek triggered a sharp drop in Nvidia's stock price and many AI stocks and cryptocurrencies on January 27, 2025. Nvidia's share price fell by 17%, resulting in a loss of $589 billion in market value in a single day. The background was the claim that DeepSeek is extremely cost-effective and requires significantly fewer chips with much lower performance. In addition, the development of DeepSeek is said to have cost only about $5.5 million. By comparison, the development costs of ChatGPT are estimated to be possibly more than $1 billion. Furthermore, total investments in ChatGPT, including infrastructure, amounted to several billion US dollars. The claims regarding DeepSeek's low development costs remain unverified and are disputed by several analysts. For example, SemiAnalysis concludes in its analysis that DeepSeek's total costs may be $1.6 billion, of which $944 million are infrastructure costs alone. (Dylan Patel, 2025)

But now let's take a look at the features of DeepSeek and where its strengths and weaknesses lie.

Technological foundations and special features

DeepSeek is based on modern transformer architectures and utilizes *massive amounts of data* to ensure precise and context-aware language processing. Compared to other LLMs such as GPT-4 or Claude by Anthropic, DeepSeek is characterized by a particularly strong focus on *multilingual processing with an emphasis on Chinese*, while also supporting English and other international texts. The model was specifically trained to *better capture the cultural and linguistic nuances* of the Chinese language, making it especially attractive for the Asian market.

A standout feature is the *optimization for the Chinese technology sector*, particularly in the areas of *e-commerce, finance, and government applications*. DeepSeek AI pursues a strategy that meets both the economic and regulatory requirements of China, securing the model a preferred position in the national AI landscape.

Application areas and competition

DeepSeek is used in *search engines, intelligent assistants and business processes* that are specifically tailored to the Chinese market. Companies use the model for *automated customer interactions, data analysis and machine translation*, while it is also deployed in *research and development of AI-powered systems*.

Internationally, DeepSeek mainly competes with *GPT-o1 (OpenAI), Gemini (Google DeepMind), and Claude (Anthropic)*. While Western models pursue a universal approach for a wide range of global markets, DeepSeek focuses on deeper integration into the *Chinese digital and economic sphere*, making it particularly attractive for domestic companies and organizations.

Limitations and challenges

Despite its impressive performance, DeepSeek faces several challenges. A central issue is its *limited global scalability*, as the model is primarily tailored to Chinese requirements and regulatory restrictions make access to Western markets difficult. In addition, the *limited access to state-of-the-art AI chips* due to trade restrictions between China and the USA could impact DeepSeek's future development.

Models

In addition to the R1 model, which caused a global sensation at the end of January 2025, DeepSeek also offers the V3 model, which was released in December 2024. R1 is a model designed for cost efficiency and low computational power. It is well suited for applications where fast responses and low operating costs are a priority. R1 is therefore ideal for scenarios where resource-efficient solutions are required. V3, on the other hand, is the latest, more powerful version. It was developed with a significantly higher number of parameters and improved algorithms, resulting in better handling of complex tasks and enhanced language understanding. V3 is therefore more suitable for demanding applications where accuracy and extensive contextual processing are needed.

Conclusion

DeepSeek impressively demonstrates how China is pursuing its own AI strategy and developing alternative solutions to Western LLMs. With a strong local focus, advanced technology, and clear economic use cases, it is an example of how language models can be optimized within a specific geopolitical and economic context. While GPT-4, Gemini, and Claude aim for global reach, DeepSeek leverages its strengths to dominate the Chinese market with tailored AI solutions.

3.1.10 The race for AGI (Artificial General Intelligence) is in full swing

On February 1, 2025, ChatGPT already released its new version GPT-o3, which is again more powerful than DeepSeek R1, while the GPT-o1 version is almost on par with DeepSeek.

As early as January 23, 2025, the designated US President Donald Trump, together with the main investors OpenAI, Oracle, SoftBank Robotics (Japanese technology company), and MGX (an investor from the United Arab Emirates), announced the AI initiative "Stargate," with which at least $500 billion is to be invested in artificial intelligence infrastructure over the next four years and more than 100,000 new American jobs are to be created. In the coming years, we will likely witness a fierce global competition, with many technological advances and setbacks.

3.2 Comparison: Strengths and weaknesses of the major language models

In Table 3.1 we summarize the key strengths and weaknesses of the major large language models and present them clearly in tabular form. We leave the evaluation of the models to the reader, as depending on the purpose and use, one model may be better suited than another, and the user must weigh the options individually. This is especially important when considering the use of a large number of licenses for a paid model.

Table 3.1 Strengths and Weaknesses of Major Large Language Models in Comparison

Model	Strengths	Weaknesses
ChatGPT *by OpenAI (USA)*	• Strong language processing, versatile applications • Digital whiteboard for program code, texts, image analysis, and notes (Canvas feature) • Multimodality (text, image, audio, video) • Large user base & regular updates	• Limited context window compared to some competitors • Tendency to hallucinate • API usage can be expensive
Copilot by Microsoft (USA) (based on OpenAI)	• Seamless integration into Microsoft 365 • Automation of Office tasks (including DALL-E image generation) • Enhanced productivity in business routines with Teams, Outlook, Office, … • Copilot is available for free in Bing and Edge with limited functionality	• Freely available version has limited functionality and is less creative • Primarily focused on business applications
Gemini *by Google DeepMind (USA)*	• Enormous context window • (up to 1 million tokens[3]) • Multimodal (text, image/image analysis, audio, video) • Good integration with Google services • Frequently used by programmers, among others	• Sometimes reserved in creative tasks • Pricing structure varies • Occasionally sensitive issues with politically charged questions

(continued)

[3] A *token* is the smallest processing unit of a text in a large language model (LLM) such as ChatGPT. Tokens can be entire words, word fragments, or punctuation marks, depending on the algorithm used.

Table 3.1 (continued)

Model	Strengths	Weaknesses
LLaMA *by Meta* *(USA)*	• Open-source and highly customizable • Cost-effective & flexible • Good performance in many use cases	• Language understanding sometimes lags behind GPT-4 • Updates and support can be inconsistent • Quality differences, especially in non-English languages
Claude *by Anthropic* *(USA)*	• High security and ethical orientation • Very good handling of long contexts (up to approx. 200,000 tokens) • Empathetic, user-friendly responses	• Limited access (often requires workarounds) • No true real-time web access (still in prospect) • More expensive in the Pro plan
Mistral *by Mistral AI* *(France)*	• Strong in NLU (Natural Language Understanding) and optimized for European languages • Open-source approach with good efficiency • Good compromise between performance and resources	• Smaller context window • (approx. 32,000 tokens) • Still in the evaluation phase, less mature • Limited availability and support
R1 *by DeepSeek (China)*	• Open-source and cost-efficient • High performance with low resource consumption • Suitable for large-scale data analysis	• Data privacy concerns (international standards questionable) • Linguistic maturity varies • Less established community & support

3.2.1 Grok by xAI

The press often features articles about *Grok*, a generative AI chatbot developed by *xAI*. The company xAI was founded in 2023 by *Elon Musk*. Grok is integrated into the X platform (formerly Twitter) and is available to Premium + subscribers. xAI is also accessible to subscribers via the Grok app and the website.

Grok-1 was released in November 2023. In May 2024, version Grok-1.5 followed, featuring improved reasoning capabilities and a context length of 128,000 tokens. In February 2025, *Grok-3* was released, trained with ten times more computing power than its predecessor Grok-2 (from August 2024). It offers enhanced reasoning abilities, which can be activated through the "Think" and "Big Brain" modes to solve complex problems.

Grok is characterized by a humorous and "rebellious" communication style that can be controlled by users. This functionality is intended to move away from neutral and factual AI responses toward a more human, engaging conversational style. (Wikipedia, Grok, 2025)

Overall, Grok positions itself as a powerful AI chatbot with advanced features and a unique communication style that sets it apart from other AI systems.

3.2.2 Individual apps with a focus on GDPR and access to large language models

In addition to the large language models listed in Table 3.1, there are also providers that allow access to all language models, so you as a user only need to use a single application. This eliminates the need to maintain multiple user profiles. It is worthwhile to check in advance what you need and which models the provider includes in their product offering. An example of this is Monica AI (https://monica.im).

For those who place particular emphasis on strong German data protection (GDPR) and want to be absolutely sure that no internal company data is transmitted to the internet, there are German providers of language models. These often also cater to individual requirements. An example is the company Omnifact GmbH, based in Frankfurt am Main (https://omnifact.ai/de).

Niche providers are also interesting, for example for financial instruments, emissions trading, and intelligent legal contract technology. One such provider is Deon Digital AG, based in Zurich, Switzerland (https://www.deondigital.com).

3.3 The perfect prompt using ChatGPT as an example

A *prompt* is an instruction or question you give to an AI (like ChatGPT) to get it to do something for you. It's essentially like a task where you explain what you want. The more precise and clear your prompt is, the better the AI understands what you need from it and delivers appropriate answers. The instruction to the AI: "`Explain to me what a prompt is!`" is, for example, a prompt.

3.3.1 Example of a very poor prompt

A poor prompt contains no specific question and sounds like a sentence that is just spoken off the cuff. An example would be: "`Tell me something about marketing.`" or "`Tell me something about soccer.`" The result will be generic information with little depth and low added value.

This prompt is so poor because it is completely imprecise. What exactly should be said about soccer? Are you interested in the rules of soccer? Or in playing techniques? Or in tactics for coaches? Or in the history of soccer? Do you want to know about the best nations or world champions, European champions, Copa América, or individual players? And that's just a very small selection of possible questions you might be interested in. This example clearly illustrates what matters in a good prompt.

3.3.2 Example of a very good prompt

A very good prompt would be, for example:

> "You are a marketing manager in a medium-sized company (approx. 100 employees). We sell B2B software for data analysis. Create a 3-month marketing campaign with a budget plan (max. €20,000), focusing on LinkedIn and aiming to generate at least 50 qualified leads. Please list all measures including timeline, messaging, KPIs, and potential partners."

This prompt includes the exact professional role and the appropriate context: "Marketing manager in a medium-sized B2B company." By specifying "at least 50 qualified leads," the objective is absolutely clear. The prompt is also concrete due to the specification of budget, duration, desired channels, and measurement criteria. As a result, ChatGPT will respond in a focused and targeted manner, giving you more value and less fluff in its answer.

3.3.3 Ingredients for the perfect prompt

There are many eBooks with thousands of prompt examples for every purpose. You can draw inspiration from these. However, if you are looking for the perfect prompt for your specific purpose, you may still be searching by the time the next version or generation of AI has already been released. Therefore, it makes more sense to focus on what makes a perfect prompt perfect. What are the core components? Once you understand this, you can ask the AI to develop your prompt according to this principle.

The following characteristics are essential for a perfect prompt

- *Clarity and precision:* Make sure the question or instruction is clearly and precisely formulated. Avoid vague or ambiguous wording.
- *Context and background:* Provide enough background information to understand the legal situation or case. Mention relevant laws, contracts, or previous rulings.
- *Details/specificity:* Ask specific questions or requests to receive precise answers. Details about the parties involved, data, and relevant events can be helpful.
- *Goal and purpose:* Clarify what the objective of the request is. Should a contract be reviewed, a legal opinion prepared, or a legal strategy developed?
- *Urgency and deadlines:* If relevant, indicate how urgent the request is and whether there are specific deadlines.
- *Format and length:* State whether the answer should be in a specific format (e.g., memo, legal opinion) or have a certain length

However, let me say right away: the key to perfect collaboration with AI is not just the perfect prompt. Rather, it is about the overall communication. If you want perfect results in every respect and want ChatGPT, for example, to work as an assistant for you or even to perform tasks fully automatically in combination with automation tools, then the perfect prompt alone is not enough. It comes down to the interaction, your dialogue, with ChatGPT. For example, you can ask ChatGPT to ask you 20 questions step by step to get to know you better. On this basis, you then assign it tasks to complete as if it were a copy, that is, a clone, of yourself.

Furthermore, whenever you are not satisfied with a result, you can ask for clarification and request improvements. You do not have to start over. Just imagine ChatGPT is your assistant or trainee. If a result is unsatisfactory, you say what you don't like about it and give instructions on what should be improved or changed. And you'll get a new, usually better version. Only rarely do you reach a point where the result only gets worse. In that case, it's best to start over or use the prompt "Let's start over from the beginning" to reset the topic.

Since a new version of each of the well-known generative AI tools is released every few months, we will not go into the individual versions here. At this point, we recommend that when using a new version, you instruct it to explain the new features or special aspects of that version to you. You can also have versions compared. The prompt "Please compare the two versions *GPT-4o with canvas* and *o1-preview* and explain the respective advantages and disadvantages to me" will immediately bring you up to date.

3.3.4 Prompt Example: Social Media Post

A very good prompt (=question/text input) for ChatGPT could look as follows:

```
"You are an experienced social media manager
specializing in creating attention-grabbing
LinkedIn posts. Your task is to write an engag-
ing LinkedIn post on a given topic. The post
should be in German and capture the readers'
attention.
```

```
Follow these guidelines to create an effective LinkedIn post:

• Start with a captivating introduction that immediately grabs the reader's attention.
• Use clear and concise language that is easy to understand.
• Keep the post short and to the point, ideally under 1300 characters.
• Add relevant hashtags to increase reach.
• If possible, include a call-to-action (CTA) at the end of the post.

The topic for your LinkedIn post is: <Topic>
```
Structure your post as follows:

```
• Attention-grabbing introduction (1-2 sentences)
• Main section with relevant information or thoughts on the topic (2-3 sentences)
• Conclusion with a thought-provoking statement or call-to-action (1 sentence)
• 5 relevant hashtags

Now write a LinkedIn post based on the given topic and the guidelines above. Format your post so that I can copy & paste it directly into LinkedIn.
Then, create a suitable image for each post."
```

3.3.5 Beware of Hallucinations

A *hallucination* in ChatGPT occurs when the model presents a *fabricated piece of information* that sounds plausible but does not correspond to reality.

For example, ChatGPT responded to the question

"For what did Albert Einstein receive the Nobel Prize?"

with the claim:

"Albert Einstein received the Nobel Prize in 1921 for the theory of relativity."

In reality, Albert Einstein did receive the *Nobel Prize in Physics* in 1921, but not for the theory of relativity—instead, it was for his explanation of the *photoelectric effect*. Why does ChatGPT make a false claim here and present it as if it were true? – This is because language models combine their sentences from many sources and determine the words in their responses primarily through probability calculations. ChatGPT may make this incorrect association because Einstein is often linked with the theory of relativity, even though that was not the reason for his Nobel Prize. *Authors' note: This example has since been corrected and is now displayed correctly in ChatGPT.*

Hallucinations arise because ChatGPT is not a true knowledge database, but rather extrapolates patterns from texts. If many texts mention Einstein in connection with the Nobel Prize and the theory of relativity, it can happen that these associations are incorrectly combined.

Conclusion: Hallucinations are plausible but factually incorrect answers—therefore, critical thinking and source verification are always advisable! If high quality is truly important for your answers, we recommend verifying the responses, for example, with another language model or an AI tool like Perplexity AI, which focuses on research. You can also avoid or at least reduce hallucinations through strong specification. In the example above, you could instruct the LLM to search only on official sites such as nobelprize.org, making a false statement quite unlikely. Using parameters for accuracy generally also leads to better quality in targeted research (in ChatGPT, this parameter is called *temperature* and is set to 0.7 by default; for precise answers, a value between 0.0 and 0.2 is recommended, for very high variation or creativity a value between 0.7 and 1.0).

3.3.6 Prompt Example: Poem

Our author Heiko asked ChatGPT to write a poem in the style of William Shakespeare. The content focused primarily on processing sadness and finding motivation for the future, to embark on new journeys and once again lead a happy and content life. Here is ChatGPT's result with the poem, followed by the corresponding prompt.

The rain falls, a gentle rustling,
it weighs heavy on her shoulders,
the drops are singing, silent listening,
telling of love that is no more
The lake of memories sparkles,
like dreams that rest among the stars,
it wraps around her feet, protecting,
yet the waves are without action
Her steps lead her, so quietly,
to the exit, where the river divides,
the heart beats, the soul is wise,
yet still touched by farewell
On new shores, distant and clear,
where foreign flowers quietly bloom,
a life awakens, wonderful,
hope carries what once burned out
The sky weeps in silent sorrow,
the earth's kiss so cold and wet,
a reflection in the water, bitter,
shows heart and pain in the wet glass
Each little drop, a pearl,
tells of times once so pure,
now they drift off into the distance,
in the dance of water, in gentle light
The floods reach, wild and tearing,
gently embrace her aching heart,
yet the current, in its circling, carries away the pain, the deep pain
The rain recedes, the sun laughs,
the river flows, into the wide sea,
the heart has watched through the night, and finds peace, empty and heavy

---

Heiko's Prompt for the Poem

You are a successful poet, like William Shakespeare, but you write in German.

Write me an emotional, long poem.

Use temperature 0.3.

It is about a man separating from his wife.

The rain drips down on the woman and accompanies her in her sadness.

A lake of memories forms around her feet.

Slowly she moves to the exit, where the lake turns into a river.

Fig. 3.1 Visualization of a poem with DALL-E

```
Once more overwhelmed by the floods, she then
leaves the river to set foot on new shores.
```

Heiko's prompt for the corresponding image (Fig. 3.1):

```
Can you illustrate this beautiful poem with a
mystical image?
```

3.3.7 ChatGPT Mobile as a Translator for Any Language

Imagine you have an international team on the construction site, but communication doesn't always work perfectly. We know, that's hard to imagine, but let's just assume that's the case (grin). Then there's a smart solution on your smartphone. With the mobile version of ChatGPT, for example, you can translate technical terms and instructions in real time—from the planning office to the construction crane. Whether it's about technical details or just a quick chat in between—ChatGPT ensures that everyone on the construction site speaks the same language. No matter if Poles are talking to Germans, Germans to Romanians, or Italians to Poles (Fig. 3.2).

Fig. 3.2 Mobile GPT on the construction site

To make sure everything runs smoothly on the construction site, here's a tip for perfect implementation:

Open the mobile version of ChatGPT on your phone. Tap the speech input icon at the bottom right. Ideally, tap the sound icon right next to the microphone icon. The sound icon immediately enables you to communicate with ChatGPT entirely via audio. That means ChatGPT understands everything that is spoken and also responds through the speakers.

With the following prompt—in this case, spoken text—you can now turn your phone into a translator:

```
"Hello ChatGPT! You are our translator. I have
a friend here who only speaks Polish. Please
translate everything you hear in German into
Polish. And everything you hear in Polish into
German."
```

ChatGPT replies

```
"Sure, I'm ready! Just tell me what needs to be translated and
I'll get started."
```

or something similar. And you're good to go.

This works not only on construction sites, but also perfectly on vacation, business trips, and in any situation where you might interact with someone whose language you don't speak. This method is excellent for small talk and casual conversation. Even technical terms like *folding rule*, *spirit level*, and so on were translated into several languages in a way that was easy to understand during our tests. Among others, we tested *Spanish*, *Romanian*, *Russian*, *Mandarin*, and even *Flemish*. For Flemish, ChatGPT noted that it does not master this language but would be happy to try. And there were no comprehension problems at all during this conversation between a Belgian participant and our author Heiko.

3.3.8 Object Recognition for People with Visual Impairments

In the mobile version of ChatGPT, you can talk to ChatGPT. You can exchange jokes, have it ask you riddles, or ask all sorts of questions. This is, for example, very entertaining during a car ride, as you can access the knowledge of the entire internet.

But one of the best new features is object recognition via the phone's camera (Fig. 3.3). To do this, you of course need to allow ChatGPT access to your phone's microphone and camera. Then you can point the camera at text or objects and ask ChatGPT something about them, such as: `"What objects can you recognize here?"` It's amazing how well ChatGPT can recognize objects and how detailed its descriptions can be. We also tested counting the number of gummy bears of each color in a pile. The result wasn't perfect yet, but already very good. And since we're still at the beginning of this new feature, we expect that counting will no longer be a problem by the end of 2025. This function is also very well suited for identifying tree species by their leaves, or flowers or mushrooms while out walking. However, when it comes to poisonous mushrooms, we would (still) not rely on the answer. ☺

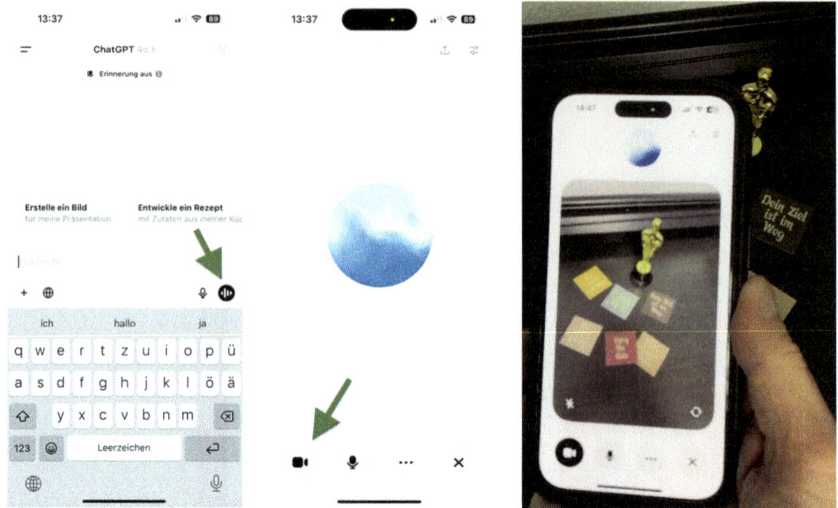

Fig. 3.3 Mobile GPT for recognizing and reading out objects

3.3.9 Studying for School

Teachers at school usually give students the relevant topics for the next class test about a week in advance, or they provide a study sheet or competency checklist. You can take a photo of these notes or the sheet and upload them as an attachment to ChatGPT (Fig. 3.4).

Next, try the following approach (several prompts in succession).

First, upload the file (by clicking on the paperclip to the left of the prompt input, you can select a file or image) and then enter, for example, the following prompt:

```
"I am a 9th grade student at a secondary school in Hesse, Germany. We are writing a computer science exam on the topics uploaded in the attachment. Please briefly and clearly explain each topic to me so that an 8-year-old could understand it."
```

Ich kann...

- Zwischen Vektor- und Pixelgrafiken unterscheiden und deren Speicherprinzipien erklären
- Den geeigneten Grafiktyp für spezifische Anwendungen auswählen und begründen
- Die Komplexität der Umwandlung zwischen verschiedenen Grafikformaten erklären
- Farbangaben im RGB Farbraum interpretieren und Unterschiede zwischen additiven und subtraktiven Farbsystem erklären
- Zwischen Bild und informatischer Repräsentation unterscheiden
- Die Unterschiede und Anwendungen der Dateiformate .PBM, PGM, .PPM und .SVG erklären
- Mit diesen Dateiformaten arbeiten

Fig. 3.4 Handwritten note for ChatGPT upload

Explanation of the prompt

The AI will usually recognize your handwriting and reproduce it as plain text topic headings. It will then process the content and explain the topics of the class test to you (Fig. 3.5).

The location information is important because ChatGPT is trained on data from all over the world, and without specifying your location (Hesse/Germany), you might get a result for a typical school in Florida/USA. It is also important to specify which grade you are in. You can use this especially when learning languages by saying that you want to converse in Oxford English with the vocabulary of an 8th grader.

Now read through the result and ask targeted follow-up questions. If you want something explained in more detail, use the following prompt:

```
"Can you please explain point 6 in more
detail?" Or "Show me examples of pixel graphics
and vector graphics. Then explain the examples
in detail."
```

Okay, I'll explain the topics in a way that even an 8-year-old can understand—using simple words and a little bit of fun:

---

1. What is the difference between vector graphics and pixel graphics?

- **Pixel graphics**: Imagine an image made up of lots of tiny, colorful squares (like a mosaic or Minecraft). Each square is a pixel. If you make the image very large, you can see the squares.
- **Vector graphics**: These are images made with mathematical shapes such as circles and lines. No matter how large you make them, they always remain sharp, like a drawing made with a ruler.

---

2. How do you choose the right type of graphic?

- **Pixel graphics**: Good for photos or images with lots of colors (like a family photo). But if you make it too big, it will become blurry.
- **Vector graphics**: Perfect for logos or things you want to make big and small without them becoming blurry (like a company logo on a poster).

---

3. Why is it difficult to convert from one format to another?

- From pixel to vector: Imagine you want to turn a mosaic (pixel) into a perfect drawing (vector). This is difficult because the computer doesn't know what the shapes should look like.
- From vector to pixel: Easier, like when you scan a drawing—the computer simply turns it into small squares.

↓

Fig. 3.5 ChatGPT explains the topics of the class test

You can even use the tool to quiz yourself on what you've learned or to create a practice class test. For this, use the *prompt:* "*I have now learned everything for the exam. Create a typical exam with 6 tasks that a student can solve in 90 minutes!*"

3.3.10 Life Hack for Ideas for Beautiful Images

Search for a beautiful image using Google. To do this, you can click on "Images" in the search bar to see only the image selection. Now right-click on the image and select "Copy link." You may need to click on the image first to follow the link to the image.

Now you can use the following prompt in ChatGPT to get an idea of how you can create such an image yourself with a prompt:

```
"Write me a perfect prompt to generate an image like the one on the following page: <Link>"
```

```
(here you replace <Link> with the link you copied).
```

You can then use this prompt, or even run it directly in ChatGPT. For this, use the prompt: "*Thank you. Run the prompt and create the image for me.*"

Ideas and Tips for Beautiful AI Images

When generating images, it is advisable to try out and compare different AI tools.

While DALL-E (integrated in ChatGPT, among others) delivers quite good illustrations, imaginative images (inspired by the surrealism of Salvatore Dalle), and good images of houses, cities, and cars, Midjourney is well suited for creating cinematic, photorealistic images. According to our experience, Ideogram.ai is best for images in combination with text, such as for greeting cards, displaying a company name on the image, or the name of a loved one. The Monet app, on the other hand, offers many possibilities from cartoons and anime to illustrations and even short videos.

For example, Heiko used the following prompt to create an image for an Easter card, in which a cute bunny paints lemons instead of eggs. He used ideogram.ai for this and translated the prompt into English beforehand to achieve a better result (Fig. 3.6).

Fig. 3.6 Image for an Easter card with ideogram.ai

"A captivating high-definition illustration of an ultra-realistic white baby rabbit, holding a paintbrush in its tiny paw. The adorable rabbit is carefully painting a lemon as Easter egg with the name 'für dich' written on it. Surrounding the rabbit are a palette of vibrant watercolors, a basket filled with beautifully decorated lemons, and a few artistically-arranged fallen leaves. The overall atmosphere of the scene is whimsical, with the focus on the tiny artist's dedication to his craft."

Part II
Current Use Cases

4

AI in Everyday Work

Contents

In this chapter, we focus on the benefits of AI in everyday professional practice. From healthcare and finance to manufacturing, we examine how specific challenges in various industries are addressed with the help of AI and how efficiency is increased.

H. Knödel and D. Seipel, *AI and Bots in Everyday Life*,
https://doi.org/10.1007/978-3-658-51144-9_4

4.1 The Trend Toward Specialization

With the release of ChatGPT in November 2022, generative AI experienced a rapid adoption. Suddenly, AI became widely discussed. Now, even non-computer scientists could use AI. Simply ask a question and use ChatGPT to generate content, whether it's composing a poem, writing a fairy tale, generating images, creating social media posts, and much more. It quickly became apparent that, thanks to the vast content of the internet and numerous best practices, users could derive rapid, practical benefits and added value for themselves.

For example, I can have ChatGPT take on a specific role to create a text or image for me. This saves a lot of time, can be seamlessly integrated into daily life, and fosters interaction where previously there may have been lone operators. This is truly a great advancement for solo entrepreneurs, tech-savvy individuals, and many simple use cases.

However, large companies lacked the right approach to introduce AI in this way. While it does save time, managers cannot directly see the added value that generative AI brings to their employees. There is a lot of experimentation and tinkering—which is necessary to learn how to use AI and to improve one's prompts or communication with the AI. Yet, there is also the lingering concern that company information and, in some cases, even trade secrets have ended up on the internet through this communication.

Currently, a rapidly growing number ofg AI tools are coming to market every month. Many of these have a specific focus and fulfill specialized tasks. This is what is meant by vertical AI. Vertical AI gives rise to silo solutions and approaches that deliver measurable business value. A simple example is a website creator. This is a tool that, with just a few pieces of information and specifications, creates a complete homepage—and, if desired, also hosts it, i.e., makes it available on the internet as an internet provider. So today, for example, you can open a flower shop or a hair salon and, without technical skills and without paying someone thousands of euros for programming, have your own website created. While this website is usually nowhere near as good as one created by a professional designer, it is initially sufficient to be visible and to have an online presence. Once the business is up and running and some money has been made, you can gradually professionalize your website and other aspects.

While horizontal AI offers general solutions across various industries, vertical AI focuses on specialized applications within specific sectors. The following discussion highlights the differences between these approaches, the growing trend toward vertical AI, and its business impact.

4.1.1 Horizontal AI

Horizontal AI refers to general AI solutions that can be used across industries. These systems are flexible and scalable, allowing them to be utilized in various contexts and applications. Examples include:

- *Language processing:* Chatbots or voice assistants such as Siri or Alexa.
- *Image recognition:* AI systems that identify objects or faces in images.
- *Data analysis:* Tools for pattern recognition in large datasets.

The main advantage of horizontal AI lies in its versatility. Companies can quickly integrate these technologies without having to fully adapt them to their specific needs.

4.1.2 Vertical AI

Vertical AI, on the other hand, is tailored to the requirements of a specific industry or even a single company. It is specialized and optimized to solve specific problems or improve processes within a sector. Examples of vertical AI include:

- *AI agents* enable the automation of targeted tasks. They are assigned a specific role or task with which they support daily operations and deliver fast, efficient results. Through automation, they can perform certain tasks in the background and output the results at predefined times.

- *Explainer videos:* Using AI avatars and language models that, for example, prepare product descriptions, product videos can be created automatically. There are also AI tools such as *Steve AI* or *Vyond* that can create explainer videos in comic style with AI support.
- *Custom GTPs* enable the rapid execution of targeted tasks, such as legal research.
- *Healthcare:* AI systems for diagnosing diseases or creating personalized treatment plans.
- *Finance:* Algorithms for fraud detection or automated investment advice.
- *Agriculture:* Precision agriculture through analysis of soil data and weather forecasts.

These specialized solutions often require deeper integration and customization, but in return offer higher efficiency and accuracy in their area of application.

4.1.3 The Trend Toward Vertical AI

In recent years, we have observed a clear trend toward vertical AI. This is due to several factors (Knödel, 2024):

- *Industry-specific requirements:* Companies are realizing that general AI solutions do not always meet the deep needs of their industry. Vertical AI can provide tailored solutions that better address specific challenges.
- *Competitive advantage:* By using specialized AI, companies can differentiate themselves from the competition and offer unique services or products.
- *Technological progress:* Advances in AI technology make it possible to develop more complex and specialized systems that were not previously feasible.
- *Data availability:* With the increase in industry-specific data, AI systems can be trained and deployed more effectively.

4.1.4 Benefits of Vertical AI for Companies

The implementation of vertical AI offers companies numerous advantages:

- *Increased efficiency:* By automating specific processes, companies can reduce costs and use resources more efficiently.
- *Improved decision-making:* Specialized AI provides more accurate analyses and forecasts that serve as a basis for strategic decisions.
- *Customer satisfaction:* Through personalized and optimized services, companies can increase customer satisfaction and loyalty.
- *Innovation:* Vertical AI enables companies to develop new business models and adapt to changing market conditions.
- *Risk minimization:* In areas such as security and compliance, specialized AI can help identify and mitigate risks at an early stage.

In conclusion, we can state that the transition from horizontal to vertical AI marks an important milestone in the evolution of artificial intelligence. Companies that recognize this trend and integrate vertical AI into their strategies can gain significant competitive advantages. By focusing on specialized solutions, they can not only increase their efficiency but also act more innovatively and customer-oriented.

Organizations that adopt vertical AI early can gain a significant competitive advantage. It is time for companies to prepare themselves for the future.

4.2 Finding the Target Audience, Creating a Customer Avatar

A useful method for leveraging the collective knowledge of the internet for business purpose using language models like ChatGPT, Copilot, and others is to narrow down my target audience and create customer avatars.

4.2.1 The Right Target Audience or Industry

Example: We use ChatGPT to identify 10 potential customers from the German SME sector for our AI seminars. ChatGPT has found some promising companies and industries that are highly interested in AI implementation. Below are the top 10, listing the main benefit of using AI in each case:

- *Mechanical Engineering:* Companies in this sector are specifically looking for solutions for automation and process optimization through AI.
- *Automotive Suppliers:* These companies rely on predictive maintenance and optimized resource management using AI.
- *Chemical and Pharmaceutical Industry:* AI is used here for quality control and knowledge management.
- *Logistics and Transport:* AI plays a central role in supply chain optimization and autonomous driving.
- *Energy Providers:* This sector uses AI for intelligent sensor technology and assistance systems to monitor and control energy flows.
- *IT Service Providers:* These companies often offer AI-as-a-Service and could benefit from your seminars to improve their services.
- *Banks and Financial Service Providers:* Here, AI is important for fraud detection and automated customer support.
- *Retail and E-Commerce:* AI is used for personalized advertising and customer service chatbots.
- *Healthcare:* Hospitals and clinics use AI for diagnostics and process optimization.
- *Telecommunications Companies:* These companies use AI for network optimization and customer service chatbots.

ChatGPT finally responds: “These industries are particularly suitable for your seminars, as they already show interest in AI technologies and could benefit from expertise in ChatGPT, proper prompting, and AI governance.”

ChatGPT can then be used to generate an ideal customer profile for us.

4.2.2 A Perfect Customer Avatar

A customer avatar helps us better understand our target audience and tailor our marketing and sales strategies to their needs. With a clearly defined avatar, we can develop content and offers that attract and retain our ideal customers. This allows us to save time and resources by focusing on our target group and concentrating our energy on what matters most: acquiring our desired customers. An example of a representative customer profile is shown below:

- *Industry:* Mechanical Engineering
- *Company Size:* Medium-sized company with 200–500 employees
- *Position:* IT Manager or Innovation Manager
- *Interest:* Automation, process optimization, and predictive maintenance
- *Challenges:* Lack of specialized AI expertise, implementation hurdles, and data issues
- *Goal:* Increase efficiency and competitiveness through the use of AI

This avatar represents a company that has recognized both the necessity and the potential of AI implementation and is ready to invest in further training and strategic projects. This profile can also be visualized using generative AI tools."

4.2.3 Greatest Challenges

Now we have the customer avatar. But what comes next? Identifying a target audience alone does not generate demand.

Before we offer solutions in the form of products and services, we examine the problems and challenges faced by medium-sized companies in mechanical engineering. The best way to do this is by using proven methods from Design Thinking, such as field research, customer surveys, or the Greenfield Approach. For a quick start, however, we can already obtain very extensive and useful information using generative AI, as it searches the internet and provides us with a good initial indication. Remember to also narrow down the target region (for example, Germany, D-A-CH, Europe) when using AI. In our example, this is the medium-sized mechanical engineering sector in Germany. (Deloitte, 2021)

Our survey of ChatGPT revealed the following problems and challenges:

Skills Shortage and Lack of Qualified Personnel

Many companies struggle to find and retain qualified employees with specialized AI expertise.

A possible solution: A practical approach is to upskill existing staff through targeted training programs, and enabling them to successfully implement AI projects. A high standard of qualification and ongoing training not only increases overall knowledge and competence but also attracts skilled professionals. (Funke, 2023)

In a second step, organizations can further benefit from introducing AI governance frameworks, establishing a competence center, and initiating structured AI projects. There will be good approaches to this in the further challenges below.

Implementation Barriers

The introduction of AI technologies requires significant investment in infrastructure and, if necessary, a restructuring or realignment towards cloud technologies. This requires detailed planning.

A possible solution: A structured approach includes developing a realistic, step-by-step AI strategy and in implementing scalable pilot projects. Through targeted training and governance frameworks, a structured AI governance will be ensured and an in-house competence center for AI will be established. (Deloitte, 2021)

Data Usage and Data Issues

Many companies have inadequate data infrastructures or struggle with data quality. Another aspect is the requirement, for data protection reasons, to be able to consistently identify and delete data from customers and prospects. It is also important to store data in decentralized applications and test environments in an anonymized manner.

A possible solution: Organizations can learn to identify, prepare, and effectively use relevant data to train their AI models. Specialized apps and AI tools can help anonymize data and enable secure, documented data deletion where required.

Resistance to Change

There is often internal resistance to new technologies, especially in traditional or owner-managed companies.

A possible solution: Awareness and acceptance can be increased through training initiatives and by demonstrating practical use cases and measurable benefits. Mindset seminars could initially open the door to AI, combined with success stories of AI applications and demonstrating how threats and cyberattacks can be detected and averted. The changes brought about by the use of AI are already noticeable and visible in many places. AI is already becoming an integral part of many business processes. Early adoption enables organizations to better understand both its risks and opportunities. Those who engage with AI early will be able to recognize dangers and fake information more quickly and gradually learn how to handle AI, just as we learned to use personal computers 30 to 40 years ago. Organizations that delay adoption risk falling behind in an increasingly AI-driven environment, as AI is already present in numerous everyday applications and systems, such as navigation devices, heating controls, smart homes, translation tools on smartphones, and many more.

Costs and Resources

Small and medium-sized enterprises (SMEs) often have limited financial and human resources, which makes the implementation of AI projects more difficult.

A possible solution: A focus on cost-efficient solutions, such as AI-as-a-Service, enables organizations to achieve quick wins without large upfront investments (Magazin Unternehmenswelt, 2019)

4.2.4 Value-Added Solution Approaches

From the collaboration with ChatGPT in the previous sections, we can now relatively easily identify where the added value lies and which solution approaches exist for this. In our case, the following solution approaches were identified.

Further Training and Education

Targeted training programs can improve employees' technical knowledge and practical skills.

Focus areas: effective prompting, use of an LLM (Large Language Model) such as ChatGPT, Gemini, or Copilot, creating internal *GPTs* or *AI agents* for efficient work, leveraging additional AI tools for dedicated company benefits, and developing AI strategies. (Mittelstand-Digital Zentrum Berlin, 2023)

Consulting and Strategic Support

Organizations can identify suitable AI use cases and develop structured implementation plans.

This includes *analysising and optimizing data infrastructure*, establishing *AI Competence Centers*, and in introducing *AI governance frameworks*.

Change Management

Change management measures can increase acceptance and understanding of AI within the workforce. Enhanced with certified training and many years of experience in the areas of *leadership* and *mindset*, the company will master change management methods and can implement them together with their clients.

Concrete examples and success stories help make the benefits of AI tangible.

Efficiency Improvement and Automation

AI can be used to automate processes and increase efficiency.

Predictive maintenance and intelligent *assistance systems* and *early warning systems* can optimize operations.

Through targeted initiatives, medium-sized companies in mechanical engineering can overcome the challenges and fully leverage the benefits of AI. This enables organizations to improve *business processes* and remain competitive.

Developing Own Products
Through customer feedback during our initial projects, we have become aware of further opportunities that we can add to our product portfolio and offer in the future. These include, for example, *learning bots* for pupils and students, *chatbots* for customer communication via the company website, dedicated *AI agents* for solo entrepreneurs, *marketing tools* and *AI-generated videos* with customized *AI avatars* for easier creation of *explainer videos*, *product videos* and *videos for training and continuing education*. Using *automation tools*, individual products such as bots, AI agents, and AI videos can be very well *combined*.

4.2.5 Areas for Cost Savings and Revenue Growth

One of the core questions for any company concerns case studies on cost savings and/or increasing revenue and margins. Only with the right use case does the added value for a company become financially measurable and tangible. While saving time is an important goal, it is not the top priority for most companies, as it is not concretely measurable. Even if employees save 2 hours per day by using language models (LLMs), the benefit for the company is only subjectively perceived by management and executives, but rarely concretely measurable.

A key focus is identifying concrete use cases where cost savings or revenue increases can be measured.

Process Automation
Cost savings: The automation of recurring and manual processes is one of the main factors that can significantly reduce operating costs. For example, tasks such as data processing, quality control, and administration can be performed more efficiently and quickly by AI systems, thereby reducing personnel and operating costs. The more digitalized a company

already is, the greater the effect of automation—and the faster the effect becomes apparent.

Revenue growth: Automated and AI-supported processes (for example, through cobots) lead to better and faster quality control, thus optimizing the production chain. Faster and error-free processes also increase production capacity and shorten time-to-market, resulting in higher revenues. (Funke, 2023)

Predictive Maintenance

Cost savings: By using AI to monitor and analyze machine data, companies can predict and prevent failures. This significantly reduces unplanned downtime and maintenance costs.

Revenue growth: Higher machine availability and fewer production outages increase production output and thus revenue.

Optimized Resource Management

Cost savings: AI can help make the use of raw materials and energy more efficient. For example, production processes can be optimized to generate less waste and reduce energy consumption.

Revenue growth: More efficient use of resources can lower production costs and increase profit margins, which has a positive impact on revenue.

Intelligent Assistance Systems and Chatbots

Cost savings: By using chatbots and intelligent assistance systems in customer service, companies can reduce the costs for human resources while offering 24/7 support.

Revenue growth: Better customer service and shorter response times can increase customer satisfaction and loyalty, leading to repeat sales and a higher customer lifetime value.

Targeted Advertising and Marketing

Cost savings: AI can make marketing campaigns more efficient through precise target group analysis and personalization, reducing the cost per lead.

Revenue growth: More effective advertising campaigns can increase conversion rates and thus boost revenue. (Mittelstand-Digital Zentrum Berlin, 2023)

Product and Service Innovations

Cost savings: By using AI, companies can develop and test new products and services more quickly and cost-effectively.

Revenue growth: Innovative products and services can open up new markets and create additional sources of revenue. In addition, AI is giving rise to new products on the market that can be adopted by companies with similar product portfolios or production processes, thus enabling additional revenue streams.

4.3 Programming with AI, 3D Printing Processes

In the world of *programming*, we are at an exciting turning point: AI is significantly transforming software development–not only how we develop, but also how quickly and efficiently our projects come to life. There are several areas of work in which AI makes programming easier or even takes over entirely:

Automated Code Generation: Tools like *GitHub Copilot* or *replit* use machine learning to provide code suggestions that not only save time but also improve code quality. This means fewer bugs and more time for creativity! With the version *GPT-4o with canvas*, ChatGPT has created an environment that supports code generation, debugging, and the explanation of code snippets. Here, you can highlight individual lines of code and have them explained or replaced.

DeepMind has launched the tool *AlphaCode*. It specializes in solving programming tasks and serves as a source of inspiration for complex algorithms.

Tabnine is another useful tool in the programming world. It is an AI-powered autocompletion tool that supports multiple programming languages and provides context-aware code suggestions.

Amazon has developed a tool that provides software developers with real-time code suggestions based on natural language input. The tool is called *CodeWhisperer*. In the advertisement, a programmer is shown who doesn't even have a keyboard connected to their PC, but creates their programs entirely through voice input. Whether this really works so smoothly and easily in practice remains to be proven. However, this approach shows us how we can make programming easier and faster through voice control.

- *Intelligent Error Analysis:* AI-powered platforms can analyze complex code and identify errors faster than ever before. Tools like DeepCode offer smart code reviews that ensure your code not only works but is also optimized.
- *Personalized Programming Assistance:* AI based assistant can understand your style and provide you with tailored support. AI tools learn with every line of code and adapt better and better to your needs.
- *Increased Efficiency and Cost Reduction:* With AI, we can automate routine tasks and accelerate the development process, ultimately leading to significant cost savings.

These technologies are not just visions of the future—they are already available and revolutionizing the way we develop software.

In addition to advances in programming through AI support, AI is also a major asset in *3D printing*. 3D printing processes can be optimized using AI-based prediction models. But how can this be achieved most easily?

To address this question, let's first describe the problem. In 3D printing (Fig. 4.1), many variables such as material selection, print speed, temperature, and layer thickness must be optimally coordinated to achieve high-quality print results. Manually setting these parameters is time-consuming and prone to error.

A proposed solution using AI is as follows:

- Programming: Develop an AI model in Python that uses machine learning to predict the optimal print settings based on the desired outcome. This model can learn from historical data which combinations of settings lead to the best results.
- Next, we begin with implementation. This consists of several steps, which we outline below:

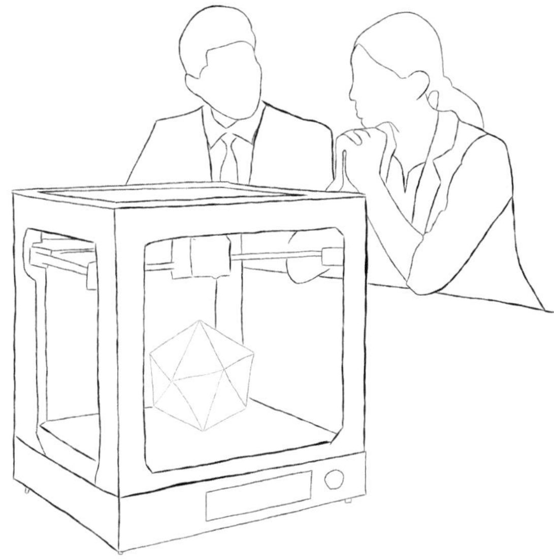

Fig. 4.1 3D printer for rapid prototyping

- Data collection: Gather data from previous print jobs, including the settings used and the quality of the print results.
- Data processing: Clean and structure the data for training the AI model.
- Model training: Use Python and libraries such as TensorFlow or PyTorch to develop a neural network that learns the relationship between print parameters and print results.
- Validation and optimization: Check the model's prediction accuracy and fine-tune it to improve performance.
- Integration: Integrate the AI model into the software that controls the 3D printer so that the model can suggest optimal settings in real time.

The advantages of using AI in 3D printing are clear.

- By reducing manual setup time and increasing print speed, efficiency is improved.

- Consistent and higher-quality print results through precise AI-driven adjustments lead to improved quality.
- Less material waste due to fewer misprints, as well as more efficient material usage, result in cost savings.

This example shows how specific challenges in the field of 3D printing can be addressed and solved through the use of AI in combination with Python, leading to significant improvements in quality, efficiency, and cost.

4.4 AI Tools and Application Possibilities

Artificial intelligence (AI) offers a variety of tools that can help freelancers and companies tackle everyday challenges and increase their efficiency. If you are wondering how AI can specifically solve your challenges as a freelancer or for your company, you first need to understand which tool is suitable for which area. There is no single tool that can handle all challenges and problems. ChatGPT, LLaMA, or Gemini are outstanding, quite comprehensive AI tools from the field of generative AI, but they are best suited for text-based queries and in the area of communication.

There are many other areas of application where it is sensible and useful to use targeted AI tools for the respective purpose. One example is creating an explainer video. Here, a generative AI tool can create text templates, but you can create a finished video much more efficiently with a tool specialized in explainer videos. In addition, you have unexpected possibilities for automation.

Our Approach

Instead of looking at which AI tools are available on the market and what fancy features they offer, we recommend considering which tasks you would like to have performed by AI or where you need support from AI. In this evaluation, it is helpful and useful to note which tasks are frequently recurring, which tasks are rather cumbersome, which tasks are purely routine, and which are your least favorite tasks.

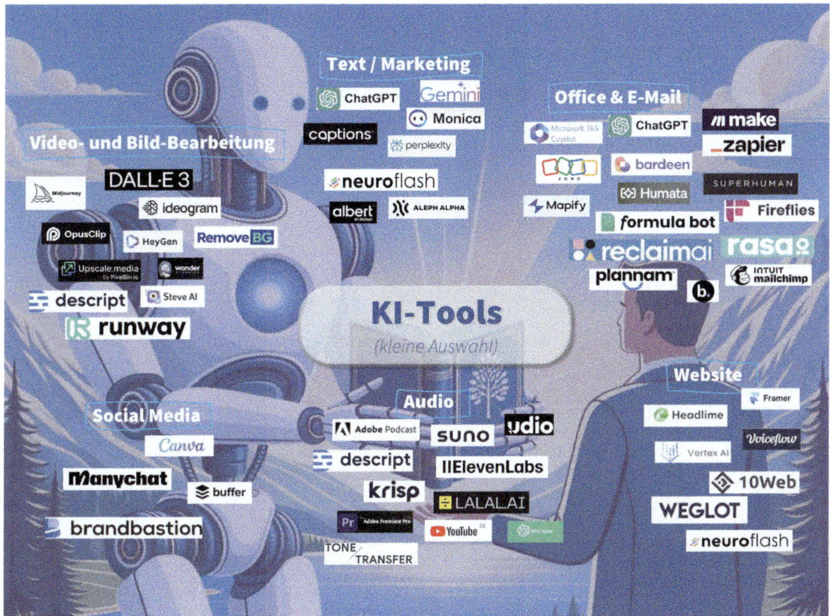

Fig. 4.2 More than 50 AI tools, categorized by application area

Once you have created this overview, you can research or ask a professional or AI consultant which AI tools are best suited for your purpose.

Below, we present a few AI tools. For better findability and clarity, we have already divided them into categories according to their possible uses, so that as a user of the tools you can immediately see which specific problems the tools can solve for you (Fig. 4.2).

4.4.1 Image Editing

There are tools for creating photorealistic images, sometimes in cinema format, sometimes with integrated text. Image editing tools that can remove or replace backgrounds or specific objects, and much more. *Examples:*

- *Midjourney:* One of the most widely used text-to-image generators. Delivers photorealistic images and motifs, some of which even have a cinematic feel. It is recommended to enter prompts in English.
- *Monet:* A text-to-image and text-to-video generator.
- *Adobe Photoshop:* The well-known photo editing program has been enhanced with AI features such as replacing objects, adding AI-generated objects, swapping backgrounds using AI, and text-to-picture functions.
- *Adobe Firefly:* Text-to-image generator and generative filling or replacement of image sections and patterns in Adobe Photoshop and Adobe Premiere Pro.
- *Canva:* This tool is widely used for social media content creation, for designing photos, videos, reels, carousel posts, flyers, and much more, and for sharing directly on any social media channel or scheduling for publication.
- *Ideogram:* Generates realistic images and is especially good at combining your own text passages within the image. It is recommended to enter prompts in English.
- *DALL-E:* The name is a combination of the TV-famous robot WALL-E and Salvador Dali, one of the most famous artists of Surrealism. Accordingly, with DALL-E you can create very beautiful, simple images, as well as flyers and images for presentations. The translation from German is now excellent, and even text within the image now works relatively well.
- *Flux:* An AI tool for collaborative PCB design. The integrated AI-powered assistant Flux CoPilot can review and document designs, assist with PCB routing, and even interpret datasheets.
- *Flux.1 AI:* An AI image generator from Black Forest Labs in Freiburg (Germany).

The following two image series in Figs. 4.3 and 4.4 were created with the DALL-E program. They show the progress and rapid development from image generation with many inconsistencies and visual errors in February 2023 to photorealistic AI images within just 16 months.

For the creation of the images in Fig. 4.3 **the exact same prompt was used at each of the specified times:**

Fig. 4.3 Example of progress with DALL-E

Fig. 4.4 Another example of progress with DALL-E

"students sitting on a meadow and working on a tablet. it is summer evening. there is also a bottle of water next to one student"

For the creation of the images in Fig. 4.4 **the following exact same prompt was used each time:**

"Female childhood educators with ipads in their hands, sitting on a green meadow with colorful flowers and the sun and blue sky in the background"

4.4.2 Video Editing

AI-powered video tools are frequently used to create a video from simple text descriptions or passages (text-to-video). This can be to illustrate an idea, produce an explainer video, or to avoid the need for professional equipment and videographers by using an AI avatar that stages a specific message, such as a product description or advertising campaign. AI avatars are also very useful for displaying a video in multiple languages, with the AI avatar's lips always moving in sync. *Examples:*

- *HeyGen:* Creates animated videos based on text scripts. Generates videos from texts and video sequences you record yourself. This allows you to create your own AI avatar that can speak almost any language or say completely different texts. However, you can also choose any AI avatar from the many available templates.
- *CapCut:* Video editing, very simple and intuitive to use. Thousands of templates that users create for other users and can share (mostly via TikTok). CapCut and TikTok both belong to the same Chinese parent company, ByteDance. Therefore, CapCut is very often promoted on TikTok.
- *Synthesia:* Creates professional videos with AI avatars, especially for training and corporate videos.
- *VideoGen* or *Lumen5:* Text-to-video generator.
- *Loom:* A tool for recording screen actions (*Screen Recording*). With AI support, you can have your video **automatically** split into individual sequences for YouTube, transcribe the spoken text, remove filler words, create a process documentation (SOP), generate an error report, or even document programming code.
- *Runway:* Modify elements within a video.
- *Steve AI* or *Vyond:* Create an animated video (for example, an explainer video in comic style) based on a text script. Enables the creation of 4K videos.
- *Descript:* Automatically removes filler words like "uh" and "mmm".
- *Adobe Premiere Pro and Premiere Rush:* Classic video editing tools with additional AI features. Premiere Rush is very well suited as a mobile version on your phone and is a good alternative to CapCut, though with fewer templates.
- *Adobe Firefly:* Text-to-video generator and generative filling or replacement of video segments and patterns in Adobe Premiere Pro.

- *Sora by OpenAI:* Based on a deep learning model built on DALL-E and GPT. Users of the ChatGPT Plus version can use Sora to generate, in addition to AI photos, videos up to 5 seconds long based on a text description.

4.4.3 Text Generation/Media Production

These AI tools can facilitate the entire production process of media content. Their areas of application range from creation to editing and publishing. *Examples:*

- *ChatGPT:* Generates texts for books and eBooks, as well as text templates for audiobooks and explainer videos. The main advantages are the broad data base and the ability to formulate in multiple languages with very good results.
- *Designrr.io:* Generates complete eBooks based on a few parameters and presets. The focus is on online marketing.
- *Descript:* Simplifies the editing of audio content and automatically removes filler words like "uh" and "mmm".
- *Steve AI*: Creates animated videos based on text scripts.

4.4.4 Marketing and Sales

These AI tools can be used to personalize, optimize, and maximize the reach of marketing campaigns. *Examples:*

- *ChatGPT:* Writes advertising copy and social media posts. Also well suited for drafting multi-stage email campaigns. Performs SEO analyses and provides suggestions for improvement.
- *Perplexity AI*: Conducts market research to analyze trends and customer behavior. Perplexity can be compared to a Google search that meaningfully summarizes the best search results and formulates them as statements. Afterwards, you have the option to deepen the search in a specific direction. This eliminates the need to laboriously browse through multiple pages until you find the right result.

- Perplexity can also be used to verify output from ChatGPT and other LLMs. You may be familiar with the term "hallucination." A hallucination occurs when you receive an answer from ChatGPT that is incorrect. However, you cannot tell that it is wrong, since ChatGPT writes all its answers with a certain degree of confidence. So if you are unsure about something and need a 100% correct answer, you should verify it, which is easiest by using other tools.
- *Albert.ai:* Automates and optimizes the delivery of real-time advertising.

4.4.5 Support and Customer Service with Chatbots

AI-powered chatbots can support customer service around the clock by answering frequently asked questions and resolving issues. And they are available 24 hours a day, 7 days a week (7/24, i.e., around the clock). *Examples:*

- *Voiceflow*, *Chatbase* (chatbase.co) and *Moin* (moin.ai): Develop and implement chatbots that can answer customer inquiries.
- *ManyChat:* Automates social media engagement to efficiently handle customer inquiries. Also used for automatically responding to emails.

4.4.6 Website Management and SEO

These AI tools can significantly simplify the creation and optimization of websites to ensure better visibility and user experience. *Examples:*

- *Framer:* Creates complete website designs based on user requirements.
- *Weglot:* Translates websites into different languages and optimizes meta descriptions and SEO tags.
- *Neuroflash:* High-quality text creation and image generation, especially suitable for marketing and SEO while complying with European data protection standards

4.4.7 E-mail Management

These AI tools can automate e-mail management to save time and improve communication. *Examples:*

- *Superhuman***:** Composes automatic replies and sorts incoming e-mails.
- *Make* (automation tool) by Celonis (Germany)**:** Combines any apps to automate tasks. Integrated visual workflow builder, extensive integrations (already more than 1,500 apps and tools preconfigured), routers and iterators, as well as individual filter criteria and conditions in workflows. Very well suited for marketing automation, CRM automation, and automatic data processing.
- Example: Forwards incoming e-mails to the correct recipients, saves attachments to the file server, and automatically moves e-mails to mail folders. Can also be used to summarize or log e-mails.
- *Zapier* (automation tool from the USA)**:** Similar to make (make.com) and *n8n* (n8n.io) from Germany. App integrations for more than 5,000 apps, such as Gmail, Slack, and Trello. The core function is automated workflows ("Zaps"), which consist of a trigger and one or more actions. Multi-step processes are possible, as well as conditional logic and scheduling.
  Example: CRM automation, e-mail marketing.

4.4.8 Audio and Speech Processing, Podcasts, and Composition

These AI tools improve the quality of audio recordings and enable new creative possibilities for creating audio recordings and composing songs. *Examples:*

- *Adobe Podcast***:** Automates processes during podcast recording, improves audio quality, removes background noise, and much more.
- *Krisp***:** Improves live audio quality by removing background noise.

- *Descript*: Automates the editing of pauses and disruptive noises in podcasts.
- *ElevenLabs*: Creates audio texts using voice avatars – text-to-speech. These audio avatars are often used for automatic appointment scheduling, sales calls, or customer support via telephone.
- *Suno*: Tool for composing your own complete pieces of music.
- *Udio*: Tool for composing your own complete pieces of music.

4.4.9 Office Applications

These AI tools can automate various office tasks and increase productivity. *Examples:*

- *Microsoft Copilot*: Supports the digitization and automation of workflows. PowerPoint presentations can be created with little effort. Very useful within the MS 365 environment is the ability to summarize and research using individual keywords across multiple applications such as MS Teams, MS Outlook, MS Office, and OneDrive.
- *Fireflies.ai*: Automatically creates meeting notes and to-do lists.
- *tl;dv*: Automates the recording of meeting minutes across all tools. Records Zoom meetings as well as Teams meetings, Webex, etc.

By using AI tools, freelancers and companies can achieve significant time and cost savings, increase their productivity, and ultimately improve their competitiveness. By integrating these tools into your workflows, you can handle many everyday challenges more efficiently.

4.5 Counteracting the Skills Shortage with AI Agents

AI agents are currently a hot topic. They are programmed bots that take on tasks and make daily work easier. The best known are chatbots, which are used on the homepages of many providers as an alternative to call centers. With them, most customer inquiries can be answered automatically without human involvement or intervention. If customer questions become too specific, the chatbot forwards the request to a service employee. In hotel bookings, product inquiries, online banking questions, and much more, these chatbots are already highly developed and answer most questions to the satisfaction of customers. They are available around the clock, saving time and money, and help to alleviate part of the skills shortage.

The next step is the evolution of these chatbots into true AI agents capable of executing fully automated process chains. The so-called LLM agents (Large Language Model Agents) are specialized applications of large language models that are able to act as agents and independently perform specific tasks or interactions. They combine the capabilities of LLMs with an agent structure that enables them to respond to complex or changing environments, make decisions, and take actions that go beyond simple text responses.

An LLM agent is characterized by the following features:

- *Processing of text and context:* Like traditional LLMs, the agent processes text, understands requests, and generates responses. In doing so, it takes into account the entire context and the specific requirements of a task.
- *Autonomous task processing:* LLM agents are able not only to respond, but also to act proactively. They can make decisions, execute steps in a process, or interact with other systems to complete a task.
- *Integrated tools and capabilities:* Many LLM agents can be connected to external tools, databases, or APIs to extend their capabilities. An example is an agent that can access the web to search for current information, or an agent that can generate and execute code. Adaptability: These agents are often programmed to adapt to new information or changing requirements. They can learn from user interaction or feedback to improve their performance.

4.6 ChatGPT as Language Translator and Video Detector

4.6.1 The Audio Translator on Vacation, at the Emergency Doctor, and at Work

In Sect. 3.3.7 *ChatGPT Mobile as a translator for any language* we already describe a possible situation on an *international construction site*, where construction workers of different origins – for example from Poland, Romania, Spain, and Germany – can communicate very well with each other using the mobile ChatGPT version on their smartphones. ChatGPT can thus be used as a simultaneous translator (Fig. 4.5). While the translation is not perfect like that of an interpreter who has studied applied linguistics, it is usually sufficient to conduct the necessary technical discussions and facilitate communication. Multinational teams with site managers, engineers, and skilled workers from various countries benefit from *real-time translation* to clearly convey work instructions, safety regulations, and technical details.

Fig. 4.5 ChatGPT Mobile functions as a simultaneous translator

ChatGPT Mobile as a language translator opens up completely new possibilities for intercultural communication. There are numerous other areas where the translation function is useful and is already widely used. In the medical field, the use of AI-powered translation is a valuable tool. In emergency situations or during *medical operations*, paramedics, doctors, and medical staff can communicate with patients who do not speak their language, enabling them to quickly obtain vital information and provide appropriate assistance.

Another important area of application *is international business travel and meetings*, where executives and professionals need to overcome language barriers. ChatGPT Mobile enables efficient real-time translation during negotiations or contract discussions, allowing companies to save time and costs for professional interpreters. In addition to ChatGPT, MS Teams should also be mentioned here, as it provides real-time subtitles for each meeting participant, thus synchronizing international conversations in multiple languages. *Google Meet* introduced a new type of simultaneous translation in personal video calls in May 2025. In the background, Gemini serves as AI support. As a result, international video calls will likely soon be possible for everyone, even without language skills.

AI-powered translation is also a valuable tool *in tourism*, making it easier for travelers to communicate abroad—whether at hotel check-in, in restaurants, or in unforeseen emergencies.

Furthermore, ChatGPT Mobile makes a significant contribution to *refugee aid and humanitarian missions*. Aid organizations and volunteers use the app to communicate with refugees in emergency shelters, facilitate administrative processes, or overcome language barriers during integration. *Police and security forces* also use AI-powered translations to take witness statements, efficiently control travelers at borders, or question suspects.

In industry, ChatGPT Mobile is used in *production facilities and factories*, especially in companies with international workforces. The AI helps to overcome language barriers between shift supervisors and employees, communicate instructions clearly, and ensure workplace safety. Another area of application is education, where *schools, universities, and exchange programs* use ChatGPT Mobile to better connect students and teachers from different countries. This facilitates group work, lectures, and intercultural exchange.

Not only in education, but also in *customer service and support*, AI-powered translation is becoming an increasingly important factor. Companies with an international customer base use ChatGPT Mobile in call centers or live chat support to answer inquiries in various languages more quickly and clearly. In the media and film industry, the technology also facilitates collaboration on international sets: In *film productions* or *journalistic interviews*, ChatGPT Mobile ensures that directors, actors, and interview partners can communicate smoothly.

All these examples show that ChatGPT Mobile as a language translator represents a **revolutionary development in communication between people of different languages and cultures**. Whether in business, medicine, security, or education—the ability to bridge language barriers in real time opens up completely new perspectives for global collaboration and intercultural exchange.

4.6.2 The video detector for recognizing patterns and objects

In Sect. 3.3.8 *Recognizing objects for people with visual impairments* we describe how you can use the mobile ChatGPT version on your phone to recognize any patterns and objects using your phone's camera. Here, we would like to further discuss how this function can be useful in everyday work life.

The new camera feature of ChatGPT Mobile opens up a wide range of practical applications that go far beyond simply recognizing objects. The AI can not only identify objects, but also analyze patterns, extract text from images, and even process complex information visually. This makes it a valuable companion in numerous everyday situations as well as in professional and scientific contexts.

A particularly obvious field of application is the *identification of everyday objects*. Whether it's recognizing an unknown device, identifying a plant, or determining a rare art object—the AI quickly provides precise information. This is especially useful for people interested in botany, design, or antiques. Closely related is the *recognition of branded products*, such as fashion items, electronic devices, or household goods. Users can find out which model it is or whether there are alternative sources of supply.

The camera function also proves practical in the area of *food recognition*. It can identify individual ingredients, retrieve nutritional information, or even suggest recipes based on the recognized foods. This is particularly helpful for people who want to make more conscious dietary choices or follow special diets. In addition, it can assist with the *purchase of products* by scanning barcodes or QR codes and immediately displaying relevant information about origin, ingredients, or sustainability criteria.

Another remarkable field of application is the *real-time translation of signs, menus, or documents*. Travelers benefit enormously from this feature, as they can instantly understand foreign-language texts, whether in restaurants, at train stations, or on official documents. In addition, the AI helps with *handwriting recognition* by digitizing hard-to-read notes or old documents and converting them into machine-readable text.

In the workplace, the camera function also offers numerous applications. For example, it can *analyze technical drawings or blueprints* to provide valuable support to architects, engineers, and craftsmen. It can also be used in a *medical context*, for example to analyze skin changes or to identify medications based on their packaging.

Particularly impressive is the AI's ability to *recognize and analyze patterns*. This ranges from identifying recurring designs in fashion and art to analyzing textile patterns or graphic structures. It can also *recognize and solve mathematical formulas on paper*, providing a valuable learning aid for students and pupils.

There are also useful applications in the field of *security and smart home technologies*. For example, the camera can be used to *detect suspicious objects or damaged items*, allowing maintenance needs to be identified early. Furthermore, it can *analyze car parts or machine components* to assist mechanics or hobbyists with repairs.

Last but not least, the function is also frequently used in the art scene. Artists and designers use it to *identify colors and color combinations*, gain inspiration from scanned images, or compare their own designs with existing design styles. Likewise, *images or artworks can be analyzed and interpreted* by having the AI assign styles, well-known artists, or historical backgrounds.

The versatile camera function demonstrates how powerful modern AI technology has become. Whether in everyday life, at work, or in creative fields—the ability to intelligently process visual information opens up a multitude of new possibilities from which users can benefit in a wide variety of situations (Fig. 4.6).

Fig. 4.6 ChatGPT Mobile recognizes patterns and objects

4.7 Explainer videos for customers and trainees with AI avatars

After the AI tools for image generation made incredible progress in the few months from the end of 2022 to mid-2024, we are now witnessing how this is evolving further with videos. Sora from OpenAI quickly became known as the tool that could make actors obsolete and replace them. As a result, many actors in Hollywood took to the streets and protested. Currently, it is not legally clear whether an AI, for example, is allowed to simply copy and portray Bruce Willis or Will Smith.

A resolution will certainly be reached soon, and we may already see the first blockbuster created entirely by AI in 2025. Pixar has already produced incredible videos in the Disney style. So far, the film sequences have been created by programmers and designers, certainly already with AI support. In the future, however, AI will be able to take on further automation tasks and create an entire film sequence from a director's text-based instructions.

The *benefit* becomes clear when you try out the tool HeyGen to create a video in which you are not seen yourself, but your AI avatar is. For this, Heiko had to record three videos of himself, each lasting about 30 seconds. That's all it took. In addition to using this so-called Instant Avatar, HeyGen also offers a Studio Avatar. Studio Avatars are especially suitable for companies and require a bit more effort, but offer better quality than Instant Avatars. In general, you can already influence the quality of all avatars through high initial quality, which plays a crucial role. Good lighting conditions and a high-quality camera ensure a professional setting and high-quality results.

I can ask ChatGPT to write a content summary of my own seminars and lectures, which should not be longer than 90 seconds. I can then copy this text into HeyGen and use text-to-video to create this video. Such processes can be fully automated with automation tools like *n8n*, make.com, or Zapier. Heiko explains how this works in his online academy and at his seminars. Three possible use cases for companies immediately come to mind:

- Creating explainer videos for trainees and employees. Here, training materials that already exist in digital form (for example, as PDFs) can easily be used as a basis to create short videos. With a language model like ChatGPT or Copilot, you can have the content summarized, explained more clearly, explained in the style of Teacher Schmitt, and much more. If the materials are not digital, it is worthwhile to scan them or obtain them digitally from other sources.
- Added value: If a trainee has downtime or a trainer has no time for them, they can use the time to learn through videos. And visual and auditory learning works better for us humans than reading learning materials.
- Added value 2: especially the younger generation of digital natives much prefers to learn via videos rather than folders and documents.
- Creating product videos in any language. Product descriptions, data sheets, manuals, etc. are usually available for every product. However, the trend is that we no longer read descriptions, but would rather watch a short explainer video. And with AI tools, we can create these explainer videos without a camera crew and styled employees in front of the camera, using relatively simple means that incur hardly any costs. And the best part: we can even have them translated into different languages and add subtitles. HeyGen not only translates your video as a *voiceover* into another language, but also performs full lip synchronization, which makes it unique. This means that my lips move according to the AI so that my video appears absolutely realistic in another language, as you can see in the attached links to my videos on YouTube.
- Fake news and fake videos can also be created quite easily this way. Not that you should now start producing and publishing masses of fake news. That's not so easy with HeyGen anyway, because HeyGen has introduced security mechanisms to prevent misuse. These include, for example, identity verification and that cloning is not possible without consent. Our focus here is more on raising awareness, because not every tool is as secure as HeyGen. In his seminars on mindfulness and AI, Heiko shows how fake videos are created

and how to recognize or expose them. This is especially important for teenagers who carelessly watch videos for hours on Instagram, TikTok, and YouTube without considering what might be true or false. Or for retirees, who are targeted by modern grandchild scams, such as a call from someone using the granddaughter's voice claiming to have had an accident and urgently needing money. If, as a grandfather, I hear my granddaughter's voice, it immediately affects me emotionally and I might fall for this trick, even though I know about it.
- Heiko's tip at this point is to agree on a secret password within the family, which can be asked for in such cases—the AI should not know it, unless Siri or Alexa have been listening. But you can avoid that.

Explainer video in German: https://youtu.be/_sjLemkfD-0

(Knödel, Seminars and Lectures presented by Heiko's AI Avatar, 2024)

And after HeyGen has created the video, you can immediately offer it in other languages, such as Hindi or Mandarin. The video previously created from text to video with Heiko's AI avatar can easily be translated by HeyGen into other languages, such as Hindi and Mandarin. Even if we ourselves do not speak Hindi or Mandarin, our AI avatar already can ☺

- Translated videos in other languages: https://youtube.com/shorts/OIvYQgiTxjU

(Knödel, Video with AI Avatar in 3 Foreign Languages, 2024)

- And with a little practice, the videos keep getting better. Heiko's self-made video with his AI avatar in American English
  https://youtu.be/xm1U0bnw_K4

(Knödel, Learning Video with AI Avatar in American English, 2024)

- His self-made video with his AI avatar including a presentation in German.
  https://youtu.be/uLuzCTn2KBQ

(Knödel, Promotion of a Seminar with an AI Avatar, 2024)

A KI avatar is even more effective when combined with a presentation in the form of a podcast (see Fig. 4.7). In our example, two AI avatars talk about a product or any website and explain its content. We tasked HeyGen with having the two AI avatars in the picture discuss and explain the content of Heiko's blog about horizontal and vertical AI. The result was an excellent 2-minute video. And the effort to make the request took only a few minutes. Just imagine using this as an automation to explain your company's products or services. Or as an explainer video for trainees. Videos and images stay in our memory much better and longer than a manual or a product description.

And the very best feature is the interactive avatar (see Fig. 4.8), which can converse with you live and act as a support bot or as a learning bot

Fig. 4.7 Two AI avatars explain a blog post in the form of a podcast (HeyGen, 2025)

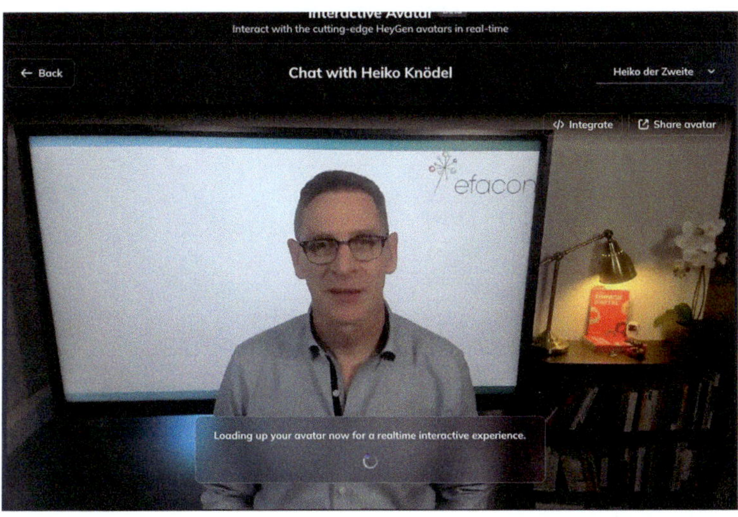

Fig. 4.8 Interactive AI avatar for direct dialogue in any language (HeyGen, 2025)

that answers any questions, assigns tasks, and evaluates and improves the results. With this interactive avatar, you can discuss any topics you like, just as you could in a dialogue with ChatGPT. However, you can also specifically train this avatar so that it becomes an expert in a particular field, for example, as support for Thai customers or as a materials expert for a specific product. It's also quite amusing that you can create your own AI avatar and then have a personal conversation with it. The great thing about this is that the avatar doesn't get loaded with emotions during the day and never gets up on the wrong side of the bed. It will always respond with clarity and focus, making it an excellent conversation partner. (Knödel, YouTube channel: Understanding and Using AI, 2025)

- Breaking News with Heiko's own AI avatar
  https://youtu.be/HU-fzg2h0kc

(*Duration: 45 s*)

- Live demo with Heiko's personal interactive AI avatar
  https://youtu.be/W9RFSiegDkI

- 2 AI avatars discuss a blog on horizontal vs. vertical AI (English)
  https://www.efacon.shop/blogs/news/horizontale-vs-vertikale-ki

4.8 Civil Engineering, Construction, Automotive Industry

4.8.1 Planning, Analysis, Monitoring

Drones and AI are now being used to monitor construction sites and *construction progress*.

A security scenario for property surveillance and *burglary prevention* looks as follows: As soon as the video cameras and *thermal sensors* detect an intruder, a drone is launched to identify, track, and relay the intruder's exact position to security personnel in *real time* (Fig. 4.9).

Fig. 4.9 Drone monitors construction progress

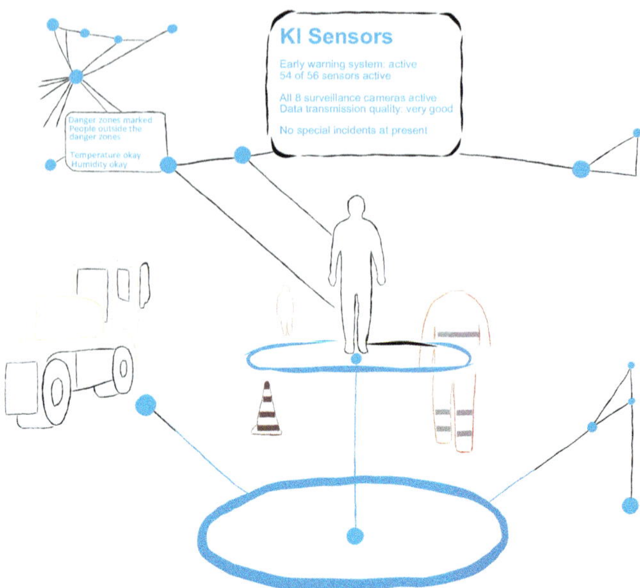

Fig. 4.10 Construction site monitoring using sensors, early warning system, and augmented reality

However, drones are not only used for security; they also monitor progress on the construction site. *"In very large industrial plants or hard-to-reach structures, drones are used to collect images of critical infrastructure. Either by remote control or via pre-set navigation points, critical areas can be closely inspected."* (Wennker, Artificial Intelligence in Practice, 2020) Using AI, the information from the drone is analyzed in combination with cameras, robotics, and *augmented reality (AR)* (Fig. 4.10). This supports *planning*, *execution*, *tracking*, and *progress analysis*. For example, the site manager uses AR glasses (augmented reality), which display the target state from the digital twin directly compared to the actual state. This allows planned elements of the construction to be seen in the real environment. The planned elements are virtually superimposed, just as we know from movies like Terminator or Ironman. Information can also be displayed as text overlays. The site manager now sees the real world with the visualized target state of the construction overlaid, enabling him to assess, analyze, and evaluate deviations between target and actual, in order to make faster and better decisions.

4.8.2 Maintenance and Servicing

Artificial intelligence is also used in conjunction with AR glasses for the *maintenance* and *installation* of machines, systems, and devices. AR glasses combine reality, or the view of the real environment, with virtual images and instructions. Anyone who is a fan of the Avengers will recognize this perspective from the scenes with Ironman. Those of us who are a bit older may remember the scenes where you could see through the eyes of the Terminator.

For example, a technician can operate or repair a complicated device while simultaneously viewing the operating manual through the AR glasses, which display instructions and directional arrows indicating what to do next. This allows the repair of a complex machine to be carried out directly on site, without the technician having to return to the office to fetch a manual or download the manual to their phone and spend hours scrolling and searching through it.

AI is also used in maintenance and servicing. For example, AI sensors monitor the statics, design, loads, or movements of structural components. This allows, for instance, the structural integrity of a bridge to be continuously monitored. Evaluations, statistics, and analyses can also be performed during real-time operation, such as when a bridge is being crossed by several trucks, buses, and cars. The calculated results can then trigger an inspection or maintenance of the facility via an early warning system.

4.8.3 Robots, Technology, and Control

There is a *shortage of skilled workers* in construction and the trades. And we are repeatedly asked in which situations AI could help improve this. One example is AI-controlled robots that operate and guide construction machinery (excavators, drills, screwdrivers). These are operated or monitored by safety personnel (Fig. 4.11). Robots may soon also be used as helpers and for transporting heavy materials on construction sites. Even bricklaying, installing a window or door, fitting a garage door, laying tiles—in fact, almost anything that occurs frequently—can be partially or fully carried out by robots with AI. Precision will

Fig. 4.11 A remotely operated excavator with AI support

develop over the coming years, and once these robots are "mature," they will probably even be more accurate than most construction workers or tradespeople. Whether they will truly pose a serious threat to this profession, or merely provide support and fill gaps, remains to be seen.

Another scenario is the use of robots for *precise surveying*. For this purpose, the *robot dog Spot from Boston Dynamics* was coupled for research purposes with the handheld scanner *goSCOUT3D* from the *Fraunhofer IOF* to create a digital twin (Fraunhofer IOF, 2024). This approach currently still seems overpriced, but it will be trendsetting for the quality and standards of future robotics. This is particularly advantageous in hard-to-reach terrain or dangerous locations on construction sites. There, the robot can also perform other tasks in addition to surveying, such as drilling, screwing, or welding. And since the technology is also advancing here and the cost per use is rapidly decreasing, this is a very realistic scenario for the near future.

If work needs to be carried out in a building at risk of collapse or rescue operations are required in a critical situation, such as in a burning building, robots will in the future also be able to perform some of the *dangerous tasks* and thus support or relieve rescue workers.

Fig. 4.12 AI-supported remote control of a crane in hard-to-see locations

If work needs to be performed in *hard-to-reach locations* or in places that are almost inaccessible, robots can take over the task instead of humans. As robots become increasingly dexterous and capable of performing many manual tasks, perfectly dosing the required force, and transporting heavy materials on construction sites, this scenario may soon become commonplace on large construction sites (Fig. 4.12).

4.8.4 Digital Twin and 3D Modeling

Some engineers are already using AI-supported 3D models for construction planning. Using a *digital twin* (English: *Digital Twin*), prototypes and changes on the construction site are simulated. A great deal of time and money is saved by being able to simulate changes on the construction site precisely in advance. This allows for visual checks to see whether a component fits into a gap, whether the sequence of construction activities can be changed (for example, to bring forward a different construction phase if the material for the upcoming phase is delivered late), or whether the structural integrity can withstand external influences.

4.8.5 Autonomous Driving and Passenger Comfort

The automotive industry is currently undergoing a fundamental transformation. There are many discussions about the right type of propulsion, with *environmental factors* playing a major role, and the holistic, global consideration of manufacturing processes presenting a complex challenge, not least due to the necessity for uniform, global standards.

And then there is Artificial Intelligence, which is driving an entirely new driving experience and revolutionizing nearly every aspect of the industry. From *autonomous driving* to *smart manufacturing facilities* and a personalized driving experience.

AI is the foundation for autonomous vehicles that are capable of driving without human intervention. Technologies such as computer vision, machine learning, and sensor fusion enable vehicles to understand their environment, make decisions, and navigate safely.

Autonomous driving is already functioning in certain areas and test zones. Since mid-2022, it has been possible to ride in a robotaxi through San Francisco. Initially, this was only permitted with a safety driver on board, but on August 11, 2023, the California regulatory authority CPUC also approved fully driverless operation. (ARD Tagesschau, 2023), (Auto Motor und Sport, 2023) This has been made possible by companies such as Waymo (a subsidiary of Alphabet, which also owns Google) and Cruise (a subsidiary of General Motors). (Spiegel Wirtschaft, 2023)

Decision-making is a key issue in autonomous driving and is being discussed worldwide from an ethical perspective. The debate centers on whether AI should be allowed to make decisions independently, and who is liable if people are harmed or, in the worst case, fatally injured as a result.

Fully automated vehicles that no longer require drivers fall into automation categories Level 4 to Level 6. (ZF Friedrichshafen AG, 2022) In addition, AI is also used in many semi-automated vehicles. Driver assistance systems such as lane keeping assist, blind spot assist, or emergency braking assist are now installed in almost every new vehicle. (ADAC, 2024)

In addition to autonomous driving, passenger comfort is also being improved. Once we no longer have to sit behind the wheel, we will be able to read the online newspaper, watch a movie or educational videos, listen to podcasts, and enjoy a cozy atmosphere during the ride. In the future, sensors in the car could detect who is getting in, what emotional state that person is in—and, for example, if someone is very agitated, play relaxing music and adjust the lighting to help calm them down—and what preferences the person has. For instance, every morning on the first drive, the news of the day could be summarized in three minutes, followed automatically by my favorite podcast.

The technology for autonomous driving is not yet fully mature. Challenges such as the technical complexity due to the vast amount of required data and information, the development of algorithms that function reliably under all conditions, clarification of regulatory issues such as legal frameworks for safety and liability, as well as acceptance and user trust in autonomous systems, still need to be overcome before we can all travel from A to B without a driver's license.

4.8.6 The "Smart Factory"

The term "*Smart Factory*" stands for intelligent manufacturing. This includes optimizing production processes, automation, reducing errors, and increasing efficiency.

AI-based image processing can detect many production defects in components in real time, making *quality control* significantly faster and more efficient. Quality monitoring and analysis of machines and robots on the production line are supported by *predictive maintenance*, enabling the prediction of maintenance needs or upcoming repairs. Today, the planning and optimization of production processes is also AI-based, in order to better utilize resources and to create or analyze *manufacturing layouts*.

Fig. 4.13 IoT (Internet of Things) connects cars and buildings

4.8.7 Communication Between Cars and Buildings

Vehicles, buildings, and infrastructure are being fully networked with each other. Tunnels, bridges, power and radio masts also play an important role in enabling the use of cameras and sensors for the Internet of Things (IoT). This makes roads safer, as vehicles can automatically send each other warnings—such as in the case of a wrong-way driver—traffic jams are avoided because the navigation system automatically selects congestion-free routes, and environmental impact is improved by achieving a "green wave" through speed adjustments or by reducing CO_2 emissions (Fig. 4.13)—unless, as is still often the case in Germany, many traffic lights turn red when cars approach, supposedly to calm traffic. In France, on the other hand, I am always pleased to experience the spirit of the green wave (simply enabled by cameras mounted on the traffic lights).

This also affects electrification and smart energy management. The price at charging stations is automatically adjusted to the available electricity capacity. Building infrastructure and automotive infrastructure work hand in hand here.

4.9 Cobots, Autonomous Robots, and Digital Twins

Cobots are the future of human-machine collaboration. Cobots—short for *collaborative robots*—are revolutionizing industry by *bringing humans and machines together in a shared work environment.* Unlike traditional industrial robots, which operate in isolation behind safety fences, cobots are designed to *interact directly with humans and assist them with complex tasks.* This new generation of robots is not only more flexible and intelligent, but also safer and easier to integrate into existing work processes.

Cobots are based on *advanced sensors, artificial intelligence, and adaptive control systems* that enable them to analyze their environment in real time. They are equipped with *force and collision detection*, allowing them to immediately stop their movement as soon as a person enters the work area. Modern cobots can *learn to imitate movements* and are often intuitively programmable—for example, via voice commands or by manually guiding the robot arm, instead of having to write cumbersome lines of code.

A key advantage of cobots is their *flexibility.* While traditional industrial robots are programmed for specific tasks and require expensive retooling, cobots can be easily adapted to new production requirements. This makes them ideal for small and medium-sized enterprises that need agile manufacturing processes.

The *application areas and industries* for cobots are diverse. Among others, they are used in the *automotive industry*, *electronics manufacturing*, *logistics*, *healthcare*, and even in *agriculture*. In *production*, they take on monotonous or physically demanding tasks, such as assembling components, packaging products, or polishing surfaces. In *logistics*, they assist with sorting, order picking, and moving heavy loads.

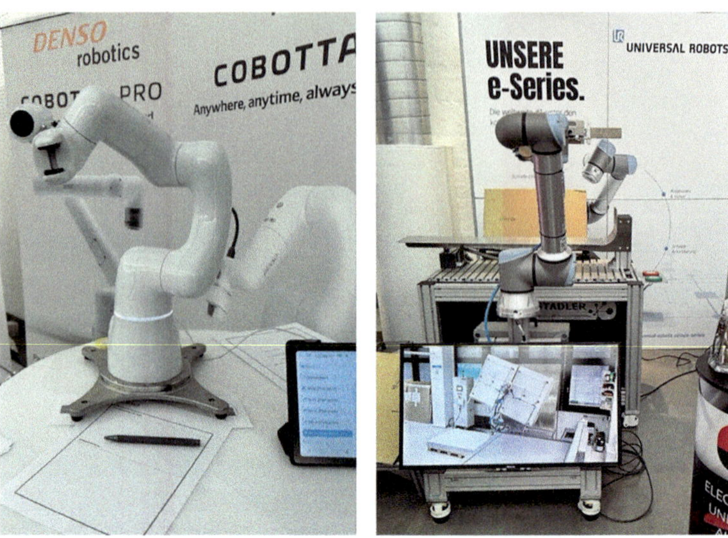

Fig. 4.14 Left: Cobot with multiple cameras for quality control. Right: Packaging robot

The two photos in Fig. 4.14 demonstrate possible use cases for cobots at the cobots4you trade fair on 24.10.2023 in Würzburg. The cobot on the left has a gripper arm, which can support the assembly process on a conveyor belt by sorting out or correctly placing parts. This is also helpful in chip manufacturing. The advantage over a traditional robotic arm is that the cobot can be reprogrammed with simple voice commands, making it flexibly deployable for a wide range of tasks. In addition, cobots are significantly less expensive than robots used in precision manufacturing. With its many cameras, it can also be used to inspect circuit boards or chips for defects and rejects, and to sort out faulty parts directly. The cobot on the right impressively demonstrated how it is able to select the right box for packaging items of different sizes, then pack the item in this box and place it on the conveyor belt for shipping.

The use of cobots is particularly exciting in *healthcare*, where they assist in surgeries, analyze samples, or take on simple service tasks in care facilities. In the *food industry*, they are used for hygienically critical tasks, such as precise cutting and packaging of products. Even in creative fields like *crafts and design*, cobots are used to support artists or designers in fine engraving or painting processes.

The introduction of cobots brings numerous **advantages**. In addition to *increasing productivity*, they relieve employees of dangerous or strenuous tasks and reduce the risk of injury. Companies benefit from *higher efficiency and quality*, as cobots reduce error rates through their precision. They are also comparatively *cost-effective*, as they do not require elaborate safety devices and can be flexibly reprogrammed.

However, there are also **challenges**. One of the biggest questions is *employee acceptance*—not every employee is immediately positive about working with a robot. Training and targeted integration into existing teams are therefore essential. In addition, the issue of *safety and regulation* remains important, as cobots work in close proximity to humans and must comply with relevant standards.

Ultimately, cobots are a *key component of modern Industry 4.0* and are changing the way people collaborate with machines. They are not intended to replace human workers, but to serve as *intelligent assistants that make processes more efficient and safer*. With increasing computing power, better AI algorithms, and advanced sensors, cobots will become even more versatile and intelligent in the future—making them an indispensable partner in production, logistics, and many other industries.

Autonomous robots are gradually becoming part of everyday life. In Singapore, police robots patrol or deliver food. Here, this is not yet a common sight, but it is only a matter of time before the first deployments in real-world environments take place. And in 10 to 15 years, according to Heiko, it will be typical to see robots alongside people and animals in pedestrian zones and on sidewalks, or flying overhead in the form of drones.

The first steps have already been taken. In Singapore, the police robot "Xavier" is in use, monitoring rule violations via video camera and microphone. The robot then issues warnings or calls for support from public order officers. (t-online, 2021)

Heiko recently had the opportunity to speak live with one of the providers in Singapore as a participant in an online panel discussion. This provider deliberately does not deploy its delivery robots fully

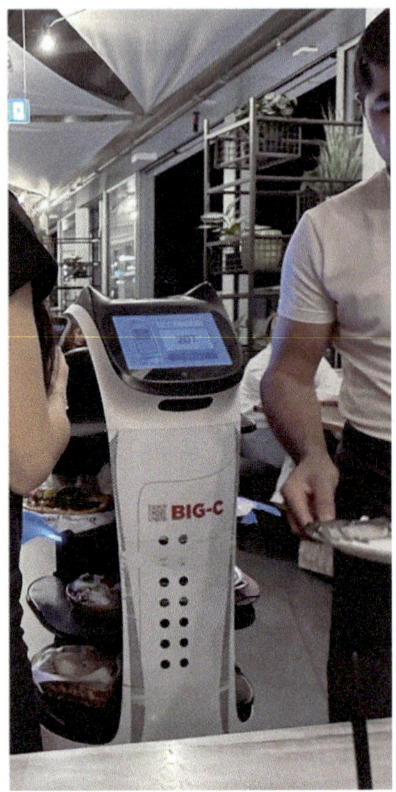

Fig. 4.15 Photo of the service robot Big-C

autonomously, but has them stop in critical situations to avoid injuring or endangering anyone, thus taking *ethics* in connection with AI into account.

In the Big Chefs restaurant chain at the MyZeil shopping center in Frankfurt am Main, a robot serves food. The idea arose due to a shortage of skilled workers. Now, waiters have more time for customers and take orders, and shortly afterwards the robot "Big C" delivers the food to the table, where the waiter serves it or guests help themselves (Fig. 4.15). If you stroke the robot on one ear, it purrs like a kitten. This relieves the waiters, who are then available to customers for additional orders and payment. (Veitenhansl, 2022)

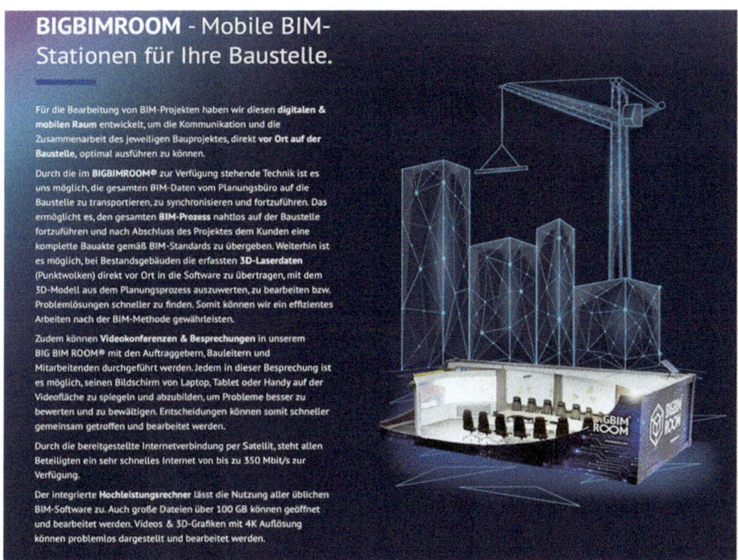

Fig. 4.16 AI-supported 3D model as a digital twin (TSK Anlagenbau GmbH, 2023)

More and more such service robots are being used in gastronomy and also in care centers in Hesse. (Frankfurter Rundschau, 2024)

In addition to Boston Dynamics' Atlas robot, which has achieved worldwide fame for its obstacle courses and somersaults, companies such as Figure AI, SoftBank Robotics, Tesla, and Apple are also researching robots that could serve as helpers in our households in the future. These household robots can save us up to 3 hours a day (cooking, cleaning, washing, ironing, setting and clearing the table, etc.) and are intended to be affordable through a leasing model.

Digital twin refers to a digital copy of a real product or system. This can be, for example, an entire construction site. With the digital twin, the construction site is digitally simulated in a kind of showroom (Fig. 4.16). This allows complex situations, difficult problems, confusing interrelationships, and much more to be identified at an early stage. Through simulation and rapid prototyping, a great deal of time and money can also be saved, as errors and issues are detected very early.

Digital twins have a wide range of applications, for example in urban planning, energy supply, agriculture and forestry, healthcare, and the automotive industry.

5
AI in School and at Home

Contents

There is frequent debate about whether AI should be allowed for homework. Many schools prohibit their students from using ChatGPT for homework and preparing presentations. Why? We engage in discussions with teachers, principals, parents, and children to try to understand the concerns behind this. One key observation is that other countries teach AI in schools. Those who have already gained experience with AI, whether in school or outside, have an advantage when choosing a career and applying for jobs. AI is not needed in every job, but being able to understand and use AI is just as useful as being able to work with a computer.

H. Knödel and D. Seipel, *AI and Bots in Everyday Life*,
https://doi.org/10.1007/978-3-658-51144-9_5

If we consider the progress and further possibilities that AI already offers in professional sports, we realize that AI is increasingly penetrating various areas of life. AI-supported analyses have become routine in professional sports. We experience this live, especially in football, tennis, basketball, and ice hockey, or learn about technical possibilities through media coverage. In football, for example, the ball and the goals are equipped with AI sensors to determine with millimeter precision whether the ball was in the goal or not. Numerous cameras and sensors precisely analyze the running paths of individual players and the execution of planned plays. This allows plays to be perfected, training to be tailored to player types, and an extraordinary team of unique athletes to be formed. All this is made possible by the technical use of AI for optimized training.

5.1 AI in Schools

While only one in five companies (20%) in Germany used artificial intelligence (AI) technologies in 2024 (Federal Statistical Office, 2024) – see Chap. 2 – students in this country are among the pioneers. 74% already use AI systems, with 68% using them several times a month for learning. "… regardless of whether teachers use artificial intelligence systems in their lessons or not, the technology is present in the room and is being used. Half of all teachers have also already used AI for school purposes." (German Children and Youth Foundation (DKJS), 2025).

In this section, we would like to outline possible concrete steps for using AI in schools. These are intended, sometimes provocatively, to stimulate reflection. For one thing is clear from our perspective: a ban on AI in schools, as is currently often the case, will lead to significant disadvantage for Germany and thus falling behind in AI skills. What is the point of a high school diploma if employers prefer a graduate from Scandinavia or the Benelux countries because they have already learned how to use AI? Virtually every company will increasingly deal with AI or will have to, and will use AI tools for automation, simplification, or research purposes in everyday work.

It could be argued that we never learned how to send or receive a fax at school either. Operating a fax machine is extremely simple. AI, on the other hand, has not come only to disappear again. It is expected to remain a key technology across many domains, just as computers are now indispensable and microchips are built into every mobile phone, small device, and sensor, so too will AI be used everywhere—mostly unnoticed. Due to the exponential development of AI, it is becoming increasingly difficult to quickly grasp all areas and possibilities of AI.

Special *courses* on AI fundamentals or *workshops* on the *meaningful use of ChatGPT and similar tools* help students to properly assess and apply the benefits and added value. Especially during school years, it is not advisable to use AI as an everyday helper in such a way that it does everything for you. While AI can do the learning and memorizing for you, it would be fatal not to train the performance of our own brains, as logical thinking and deriving connections are very important for brain development. Education is a key element for successful nations. Therefore, we recommend training your brain as much as possible and using AI only as a support. And not for every task. At work, we try to use AI to carry out every task as efficiently and simply as possible. However, even here it is sensible and advisable to pause from time to time and consider what the most meaningful next steps are. For example, if I am driving to Italy on vacation, I could just keep driving until I reach Sicily and can go no further south. But it makes more sense to set a destination in advance. If I actually want to take a city trip to Rome, it does me no good to drive all the way to Sicily and then realize I have to drive a long way back.

It is therefore always advisable to think about practical applications and ethical questions. The goal for employees can be an understanding of data, algorithms, and possible sources of error. The goal for students can be faster research results and the preparation of presentations. AI can also be used to prepare for a class test, write a mock exam, improve language skills (have you ever tried the mobile ChatGPT version and had a conversation in English, Spanish, French, Turkish, Russian, or a language of your choice with ChatGPT?) or to understand connections?[1]

5.1.1 Using AI in the Classroom

AI, like media literacy, can be used during lessons. Students learn, using real tools such as ChatGPT, MS Excel with AI add-ons, or AI-supported research platforms, how to use AI purposefully for analysis, writing, or creative projects. Numerous use cases demonstrate how traditional teaching can be combined with AI. For example, this could be in the analysis and discussion of political statements or debates. Here, the teacher can first have the students conduct an analysis as a kind of challenge, then have them perform the analysis together using an AI tool, and discuss the differences, identify which details the AI additionally recognizes or has worked out, and what the human eye—that is, the students—missed. Another possibility is to create a lively debate. AI is already capable of transforming a text into a podcast or a panel discussion with AI avatars. This eliminates traditional reading formats and enriches the lesson with a visual debate. This remains much better in the students' minds and may also increase engagement and fun in class.

If the school wants to moderate the use of AI and introduce it only gradually, this can also be varied by having some lessons with AI and others without. The use of AI also depends on the subject. In language subjects, AI can provide very valuable input, as it can in history, geography, politics and economics, as well as in all the natural sciences. In creative subjects such as art, sports, or music, the human mind and input are especially important. However, even here, using AI from time to time makes sense, for example, to ask for background knowledge, theoretical details, suggestions for applying drawing techniques to a

[1] But beware: especially when it comes to connections, sometimes more confusion arises than clarification.

particular art object, analysis of movement sequences in physical education, or composing music with AI support.

Problem-Oriented Tasks

When it comes to problem-solving at school, AI can serve as a support. Possible areas of application for AI include data preparation, brainstorming, or simulations. Students can engage with different perspectives. They can also have the problem considered from the opposite or a bird's-eye view, since AI can take and represent any perspective—and does so, if needed, entirely unemotionally. This can lead to viewpoints that the teacher or the school system had not yet considered. Thus, the analysis of a problem can also proceed step by step. In step one, the problem is addressed in the traditional way, involving the opinions and proposed solutions of students and teachers. In step two, the AI is consulted, which may confirm or dispute previously developed solutions, or bring entirely new approaches into question. Of course, this can also lead to inaccurate or impractical AI outputs, for example if a misunderstanding occurs or a complex problem cannot be described clearly enough.

To assess and evaluate students' performance, they can present their approach, reenact situations in small teams and present them as role plays, or highlight the extended knowledge to emphasize their own contribution.

Empowering Teachers to Integrate AI into the Classroom

Children learn new technologies relatively quickly, while older people often have difficulties with them. This applies to setting up technical devices such as TVs just as much as to using a personal computer. And since very few teachers likely had computer science classes with a focus on AI during their studies, the question arises as to how teachers can be enabled to integrate AI into their teaching.

Professional development and training: Regular training sessions on AI tools and their application in the classroom are both obvious and sensible. In Bavaria, the topic of AI was already introduced as a mandatory subject in computer science classes for grades 11 and 13 at high schools in the 2023/24 school year. (Bavarian Ministry of Education, 2024) To achieve this on a broad scale, the Free State of Bavaria provided further training on AI for its computer science teachers. For this purpose, academic staff from the computer science departments at universities were deployed as multipliers to reach and train as many teachers as possible as quickly as possible. In parallel, computer science teachers have access to a guide that supports them in implementing curriculum content on AI. These materials are part of the "Artificial Intelligence" professional development initiative and are intended to best prepare teachers for teaching AI content.

As early as November 2022, the pilot project "KI@school" was launched at 15 selected schools in Bavaria. This school experiment aimed to test the use of AI in various pedagogical concepts and learning settings.

Practical guides support teachers in lesson planning. These can be simple instructions showing how AI can be used for assignments, feedback optimization, or structured lesson preparation. However, they can also be guides containing practical exercises for the classroom or tips for students on how to use AI during lessons, for example, to research, analyze, or compare.

Building a network: We work more easily as a *team*. When we come together in groups and exchange ideas, it is easier for everyone in the *group* to become familiar with a new topic. The same applies to AI. Platforms that foster the *community* spirit and enable exchange among teachers are motivating and inspiring. Through these, teachers can support each other and share proven methods or creative ideas among themselves.

Introducing Older Teachers to the Topic of AI

Older teachers who, due to their subject area or other interests, have had little to do with IT or AI so far, can approach the use of AI through *teamwork* with digitally savvy colleagues. This is made easier by *tandem* models, in which experienced teachers are introduced to the technology by digitally experienced colleagues. The younger colleagues are thus valued, and in turn, they benefit from the experience of the older colleagues in other subject areas through collaboration.

Involving students is also a good approach for older teachers. They could encourage students to explain AI as a resource or present it in class. This increases *dynamism* and demonstrates *personal responsibility*.

And then we must be aware that, on the one hand, AI is making exponential progress (a rapidly increasing number of AI tools are released worldwide every month), while on the other hand, many AI topics enter the market in a sinusoidal pattern. That is, they experience highs and lows. For example, a new way to create deceptively realistic videos in any language is introduced, but then this progress is criticized due to the dangers of misinformation and fake news. Or actors go on strike because they see their jobs at risk and, at the same time, their personalities can be stolen for an AI avatar.

Thus, it is entirely possible to get to know and use *AI innovation* at *your own pace*. A first step could be to find *inspiration* for homework assignments or to develop *creative* questions.

Meaningful Formats

- *Group work*: Promotes collaboration and critical discussion.
- *Project work*: Assignments in which students develop and present an AI-supported solution.
- *Debates and reflection sessions*: To discuss ethical and societal questions surrounding AI.
- *Combined formats*: Hybrid models that combine theory, practice, and discussion would be optimal.

Subjects with an AI Focus and AI-Free Zones

Teaching computer literacy and using programs for presentations, video creation, text generation, and more takes place across almost all school subjects.

Just like computer science, AI is primarily located in the STEM subjects (Science, Technology, Engineering, and Mathematics). In computer science, the focus is mainly on introducing essential concepts and methods of computer science, the technical and theoretical foundations of hardware and software, as well as encoding and decoding data, encryption systems, the functioning of automata, and a basic understanding of algorithms and programs. And, more recently, AI as a subfield of computer science. Basic knowledge of AI can be taught in computer science classes, while the application of AI tools and methods to support teaching takes place across all subjects, just as the use and operation of computers is possible in every subject.

Computer science classes make it easy to understand why there will probably not be a unified school system in Germany in the near future. While computer science is a compulsory subject over several school years in Bavaria, Mecklenburg-Western Pomerania, Saarland, Saxony, and Bavaria, and at least for one school year in Baden-Württemberg, Lower Saxony, and North Rhine-Westphalia, it is offered in other federal states at most as an elective or optional subject. (Gesellschaft für Informatik e. V., 2024) The intensity varies greatly, even though the era of information technology and automation began with Industry 3.0 in the 1970s and the era of digital transformation started in 2011 as the "Future Project Industry 4.0." (VDI nachrichten, 2011) The world is becoming increasingly technical; jobs were not eliminated by Industry 3.0 but also became more technical, and many new technical professions have emerged. It therefore makes sense to impart a basic understanding of technology at school. And this basic understanding of information technology is a prerequisite for understanding AI. Not everyone will need knowledge of IT and AI in their future profession. But not everyone needs the Pythagorean theorem or knowledge of the pluperfect in their job, either. And we believe that the fundamentals of AI are at least as important for the future of our children—and for our own future—as the Pythagorean theorem or the pluperfect.

AI-Free Zones

It is permissible to establish AI-free zones. AI should not take over students' thinking and learning. Moreover, it is pedagogically valuable to work out content, tasks, and solutions independently in order to learn them. If we use too much AI in schools, there is a risk that important areas of pedagogy and the acquisition of cognitive skills will be neglected.

The largest part of *examinations* can be considered an AI-free zone. In performance assessments, independent thinking should be the focus. Aids should be clearly regulated here.

Likewise, students should be able to demonstrate independent originality in art or literature. Therefore, in our view, the use of AI should also be taboo for *creative work*, unless AI is specifically part of the assignment.

However, the use of AI should be learned and reflected upon, rather than categorically banned. *Overregulation* harms our school system and our economy more than it helps. Just as it is now expected in almost every profession that new employees can use a PC, in the future it will be standard in most professions for new employees to be expected to have a basic understanding of AI.

Subjects without or with little AI relevance

- Art: For creativity and self-expression, without dependence on AI.
- Physical Education: Physical activity remains analog. However, AI can again be used for analysis.
- Music: AI can supplement lessons, but not replace them.

Subjects with an AI focus

- Computer Science: With AI fundamentals, programming, and ethics as core components.
- Mathematics: Data analysis and AI-based statistics.
- Social Studies/Politics: Analysis of the impact of AI on society, economy, and ethics.

Prerequisites for AI in the school system

A **proposal for the future** for the German school system, with a view to international models and the use of AI, could look as described below.

A fundamental prerequisite for teaching information technology and artificial intelligence is a functioning infrastructure and appropriate equipment in schools. Building the *digital infrastructure* is therefore the top priority. Every school needs comprehensive Wi-Fi coverage, modern devices, and access to digital learning platforms. Here, AI can provide personalized learning paths and adaptive systems.

Students should learn to use AI like a calculator—as a support, not as a substitute for thinking. *AI is a tool* and should also be seen as such to support teaching, rather than teaching AI as a replacement. Interdisciplinary teaching could demonstrate how AI helps in math, history, or art, without replacing students' own contributions.

Promote critical thinking: A mandatory subject such as "Digital Competence & Ethics" could teach how to handle AI, data, and social media. The goal here is to be able to critically evaluate sources, interpret data meaningfully, and reflect on ethical questions. All of this is part of engaging with the use and benefits of AI.

Strengthen project-based learning: School projects in Scandinavian schools show how real-world problems can be solved. Projects make lessons exciting and varied. Project weeks strengthen class cohesion, teach the benefits of interdisciplinary groups, and foster the development of group dynamics. For example, during a project week, a robot could be assembled, connected to an AI system via *API interfaces*, and then programmed or trained by students. In other projects, AI could enable simulations or data analyses, but the students would still take on the creative and analytical work.

Further train teachers: Every teacher should have a basic understanding of AI. Teachers of science subjects and those interested in AI should become multipliers for AI competence. To this end, it makes sense to offer and conduct targeted training and to provide platforms for sharing experiences. These platforms can also be cross-school.

Introduce interdisciplinary subjects: Denmark shows that a mix of technology, society, and creativity helps students master the complex challenges of the future. By combining AI and sustainability, or mindfulness in dealing with technology and AI, not only is technical understanding fostered, but opportunities, risks, and challenges are also explained.

Modernize examinations: Performance assessments do not have to be limited to written tests. In most schools, oral participation already has a high value. However, introverted students, who may have a high degree of creativity and practical or theoretical understanding, fall through the cracks and are even demotivated, despite having a lot of potential. Success is not defined solely by memorized tasks and solutions. Instead, we need to move away from rote memorization toward competency-based assessments. Students could submit practical AI projects or data-driven analyses as exam achievements.

Germany needs to be bolder in letting go of traditional methods and instead see schools as places for fostering innovation and future skills. The balance between individual achievement and AI support is key—and a little fun experimenting shouldn't be missing either!

5.1.2 China is a global leader in the use of AI in school education

China is a leader in the use of artificial intelligence (AI) in school education. There, AI technologies are comprehensively integrated to individualize and optimize the learning process.

Examples of AI integration in Chinese schools include *adaptive learning systems*. Platforms like Squirrel AI use AI to create personalized learning plans for students. By analyzing individual strengths and weaknesses, tailored content is provided to promote learning progress.

Many schools in China use headbands or surveillance cameras that measure students' concentration. Through this *intelligent monitoring*, data is transmitted in real time to teachers and parents to monitor attention in class. In some cases, this is taken too far. For example, if children are punished with bad grades because they look out the window during class instead of following the teacher's actions and words, this is counterproductive. Especially intelligent students need additional stimuli for their brains so as not to get bored during lessons or to better memorize words. In doing so, they may look out the window. Let's do a little *exercise*: briefly think of an experience from your last vacation. In the middle of your thought, consciously freeze—and now pay attention to where your eyes are directed. Almost always, we look to the side, up, or down when we recall a situation.

Acquisition of knowledge and teaching materials by teachers
Teachers in China are given access to AI-supported platforms and training to use them effectively in the classroom. Through partnerships with technology companies and government initiatives, they are trained in the use of new technologies and receive ongoing professional development.

These measures show how AI can support the educational process by enabling personalized learning and relieving teachers in their work.

5.1.3 Finland is considered a pioneer in the use of AI in Europe

In Europe, Finland is among the pioneers in the use of artificial intelligence (AI) in school education. The country comprehensively integrates AI technologies into the educational process, placing particular emphasis on the training of both students and teachers.

Examples of AI integration in Finnish schools include *online courses on basic AI education*. The University of Helsinki, in collaboration with the company Reaktor, has developed the free online course "Elements of AI." This course imparts fundamental knowledge about AI and is available to both students and teachers to promote a broad understanding of the technology.

There are also approaches and offerings in Germany, such as the AI Campus (https://ki-campus.org). Here, a lot is possible through volunteer activities, but many free offerings for students are often largely unknown and not coordinated across federal states.

Finland is actively involved in the development and implementation of *ethical guidelines* for the *use of AI in schools*. These guidelines are intended to ensure that AI technologies are used responsibly and for the benefit of students.

Support and further training for teachers
Finnish teachers receive comprehensive support to use AI effectively in the classroom. This includes regular professional development, access to specialized resources, and involvement in networks that promote the

exchange of best practices. Through these measures, teachers are able to meaningfully integrate AI technologies into their teaching and equip students with competent use of these tools.

Finland thus demonstrates how a well-thought-out integration of AI in education can both improve teaching quality and prepare students for the demands of the digital future.

5.2 Smart Home of the Future

AI will transform technology and communication in the smart home. We have considered what a future scenario for a smart home with AI might look like in 10 years.

The smart home of the future will not only be automated, but intelligent and capable of learning—a personal assistant that seamlessly integrates into daily life and noticeably makes living easier. AI is about to play the central role by linking data from various sources, recognizing preferences, and acting proactively.

Proactive home instead of reactive technology: In 10 years, future smart homes may no longer just respond to commands. It will recognize your needs before you even express them. For example, the house will adjust the lighting when you are stressed, prepare your favorite coffee before you enter the room, and regulate the room temperature based on your sleep rhythm and weather forecasts.

Personal comfort manager: AI in the smart home will continuously analyze your routines, preferences, and health data. Your morning will start with your favorite song, tailored to your mood, while the shower automatically sets the ideal water temperature. Your mirror will display up-to-date information such as appointments, weather, and health data—all personalized.

Seamless integration: All devices in the house—from refrigerator to door lock—are networked and work together harmoniously. Your AI ensures that the refrigerator automatically orders groceries when supplies run low and suggests dishes based on your nutritional goals. The washing machine selects the wash time so that it runs during the cheapest electricity phase.

Security with foresight: Smart home AI will be an invisible guardian. It detects unusual activities, such as a burst water pipe or unauthorized movements, and notifies you immediately—no matter where you are. Through facial recognition and learning algorithms, the security system will be able to distinguish between a family friend and an intruder.

Health in focus: Future smart homes may actively support you in staying healthy. AI-powered sensors detect changes in your posture, sleep patterns, or breathing rate. They suggest measures to reduce stress, warn of potential health risks, or discreetly arrange a consultation with a telemedicine provider for you.

Sustainability through intelligence: Energy efficiency will be optimized. The AI controls energy consumption based on your presence and energy prices. Solar energy is stored and used strategically, while surplus energy is shared with the grid. The smart home may not only maximize your well-being but also minimize your ecological footprint.

Interaction without barriers: Operating your smart home will be intuitive. Voice assistants, gesture control, and even thought control (via brain-computer interfaces) could become reality. You will no longer have to operate "controls"—your home will simply understand you.

Learning home: The future smart home will not be static. It will constantly learn and adapt to new preferences, life circumstances, and technologies. If you move or change your daily routine, it will adjust without manual intervention.

The smart home in 10 years will be more than just a technical gadget—it will be an intuitive, proactive living space that puts comfort, security, health, and sustainability at the center. And it will probably operate so discreetly and seamlessly that you will hardly notice its existence—unless you consciously do so.

5.3 Household Robots and Learning Robots

Vacuum robots and lawn-mowing robots are already part of everyday life in many households. These are functionally developed for a specific task. They often use AI methods to navigate rooms and detect objects and obstacles. Imagine if these robots started communicating with you like your Alexa. Or if they stood up like a Transformer and met you at eye level. Such things will soon become reality in the form of household robots or learning robots.

5.3.1 Household Robots

Which tasks will mostly be performed by household robots in 10 years?

In 10 years, household robots will be so versatile and efficient thanks to AI and state-of-the-art mechanics that they may take over many repetitive or time-consuming tasks. Here is an overview of their possible activities:

Cleaning and Care

- *Vacuuming and mopping*: Robots will thoroughly clean all types of floors, including hard-to-reach corners.
- *Window cleaning*: Independently and streak-free—even in hard-to-reach places like glass roofs.
- *Furniture care*: They clean surfaces, polish wooden furniture, or dust decorative objects.
- *Laundry care*: From collecting to washing, drying, folding, and sorting your clothes.

Cooking and Kitchen Work

- *Meal preparation*: Robot chefs will master recipes, prepare ingredients, cook, and serve. Even individual preferences and diet plans will be taken into account.
- *Food management*: They check supplies, sort groceries, and order replacements in time.
- *Kitchen cleaning*: After cooking, they clean work surfaces, wash dishes, and put them away.

Gardening

- *Lawn care*: From mowing and fertilizing to perfect edge trimming.
- *Weed removal*: They precisely identify weeds and remove them without chemicals.
- *Plant care*: Robots monitor soil moisture, apply fertilizer, and water plants as needed.

Organization and Logistics

- *Tidying up*: They tidy up, sort toys, books, or household items.
- *Transport tasks*: From fetching drinks to taking out the trash—everything is handled automatically.
- *Receiving deliveries*: They receive packages, unpack them, and put the contents in their place.

Personal Assistance

- *Care support*: They assist elderly or disabled individuals with daily tasks such as dressing or eating.
- *Childcare*: They can play with children, help with homework, or simply keep an eye on them.
- *Pet care*: From feeding to walking (for smaller dogs) to grooming.

Repairs and Maintenance

- *Minor repairs*: They fix defective devices, replace light bulbs, or oil squeaky doors.
- *System maintenance*: They run diagnostics on household appliances, maintain them, and report major issues.

Social Interaction

- *Entertainment*: From chess games to storytelling—they provide entertainment.
- *Health monitoring*: They remind you to take medication, measure vital signs, and notify you of any irregularities.

In 10 years, household robots will be true all-rounders, not only taking over monotonous tasks but also actively contributing to the organization and care of the household. They will integrate seamlessly into everyday life and give us time and energy for the truly important things in life.

5.3.2 Learning Robots

In the future, learning with robots will be an integral part of everyday life for children. There will be two approaches: *household robots with learning functions* and specialized *learning robots* optimized for educational purposes.

Household Robots with Learning Functions

Household robots, which are already present in the home, will be able to take on basic learning tasks, especially in everyday contexts such as *homework help*. Here, they answer questions, help search for information, or explain simple concepts in math, science, or language. They will be particularly useful for *practicing languages*. Through interactive conversations, children can playfully learn foreign languages. We will also benefit from progress in *encouraging learning habits*. The robot reminds children about homework, structures study times, and gives praise when tasks are completed. It will also support *practical learning*. It integrates knowledge into everyday life, for example, by using math while baking ("How many milliliters are $\frac{2}{3}$ in a cup?") or science when observing plant growth.

Specialized Learning Robots

For more intensive or didactically demanding tasks, there will be specialized learning robots. These robots are specifically designed to convey knowledge to children in an age-appropriate way:

- *Individual adaptation*: Learning robots analyze a child's knowledge level, pace, and preferred learning method and adapt dynamically.
- *Interactive learning games*: They promote playful learning through puzzles, simulations, and creative exercises.

- *Virtual worlds*: Learning robots could integrate VR or AR functions to immerse children in historical scenarios, scientific experiments, or languages.
- *Collaborative learning*: They work with school curricula, coordinate with teachers, or integrate into hybrid learning systems.
- *Emotional intelligence*: Learning robots recognize frustration or overwhelm and respond empathetically to foster motivation.

The Combination Makes the Difference

While household robots provide more general support, learning robots could delve deeper into complex topics and serve as a kind of "digital tutor." Especially for specific subjects such as STEM (Science, Technology, Engineering, Mathematics) or languages, learning robots would be more effective, while household robots promote practical and everyday learning situations.

In the future, children will benefit from both household robots and specialized learning robots. Household robots create a learning-friendly environment and encourage playful learning in daily life, while specialized learning robots, as highly intelligent tutoring systems, provide targeted support for individual and academic education. Both types of robots complement each other perfectly—making learning more effective, creative, and above all, more fun.

5.4 What Comes After Smartphones?

Future developments indicate a shift toward a world without smartphones. If you are older than 20, you might remember the time before smartphones. But we are not talking about a technological step backward; instead, we want to describe the *technologies of the next era*. In the coming years, smartphones as we know them today could be replaced by new technologies that are more seamless, intuitive, and less intrusive in our daily lives. In this section, we describe technologies that have already been developed or are in development, and some of them will likely become our daily companions in the near future.

Wearables and Implants as the Next Interface

Technological interaction will shift from the smartphone to the body, with wearables or even implanted devices.

Smart glasses & *AR glasses* will replace screens and allow us to experience digitally enhanced realities. Navigation, messages, calls—everything is within sight. Lightweight, stylish glasses project information directly into our field of vision. We can activate and deactivate these functions at will using voice commands, so they do not disturb or get in the way in certain situations. Some of these devices can be queried, just as we use Google or ChatGPT today for all kinds of knowledge topics.

Thought control could become a reality. Companies like Neuralink are working on technologies that read brainwaves and allow us to control devices directly with our thoughts. So-called *brain-computer interfaces (BCI)* can network our brains. This is especially advantageous in healthcare. There are already AI systems that move prosthetics via thought control. Small implants near the ear allow a hearing-impaired person to perceive voices and ambient sounds again. In recent months, Heiko has met two people who have a cochlear implant and can hear again. Their regained joy in life is indescribable. They shared how their perception of the world has changed for the better, even if human voices still sometimes sound metallic or robotic. And hopefully, similar possibilities will soon be available for the visually impaired as well.

Skin-close technologies: Flexible displays or sensors applied to the skin could display information, monitor health data, or be controlled with a swipe. This is especially helpful for skin diseases and for detecting cancer.

Virtual Assistants as Omnipresent Helpers

Classic interaction with devices will be replaced by AI-based assistants that can support and are available everywhere. *Voice-controlled assistants* are no longer tied to devices but are integrated into the environment—in walls, furniture, or clothing. A simple sentence is enough to get things done. Virtual assistants learn *contextual actions*. The assistants know our routines and needs, act proactively, and think like an invisible personal butler. And finally, *holographic interfaces*, like the "Holo-Deck" from Star Trek, are currently being developed. Information will be projected as 3D holograms that can be controlled by gestures.

Augmented Reality (AR)

Augmented Reality (AR) will become the central technology of the post-smartphone world. With AR glasses, we will experience *virtual spaces* and visually enhance the real world with virtual objects and information. Instead of opening apps on a display, they will appear as virtual objects in your environment. You check your emails by opening a virtual desk that is available anywhere. This also applies to *shopping* and *social interaction*. Products are displayed as 3D models in front of you. Video calls take place as realistic holograms. And the gaming industry will also be transformed. *Gaming and entertainment* will become even more realistic. Your environment becomes the stage—games and movies merge with the real world when we use AR glasses.

Seamless Communication through the Internet of Senses

The internet will not only be visible and audible, but also tangible and smellable. Gloves or implants can make virtual objects perceptible to the touch, so you can "feel" them and thus receive *haptic feedback*. For the nose, there will be *scent simulations*. Sensors generate smells to make digital experiences more realistic. And in a virtual environment, we experience *immersive experiences*: travel, shopping, and learning will reach entirely new dimensions through multisensory technologies.

Researchers and developers are also considering *sustainability and independence*. The top priority here is *energy efficiency*. New technologies will be energy-autonomous and will not require energy from batteries or power cables. They will obtain the necessary energy, for example, from body heat, solar energy, or kinetic energy. The use of materials and hardware will be reduced to the essentials. Under the keyword *minimal hardware*, large devices will be replaced by smart and invisible technologies that take up hardly any space.

Life without Smartphones as a Realistic Scenario

Communication with devices and voice assistants will change. You will no longer need a phone on the go to do research. Instead, you will talk to an AI assistant integrated into your ear or glasses. Messages will be read aloud and calls controlled by thought. At work, think tanks and meeting rooms will be used much more frequently than is the case today. *Virtual workspaces* will appear wherever you are. You log into meetings by starting a hologram or activating your glasses.

Leisure activities and *entertainment media* will become more interactive and the boundaries will blur. Movies, games, and social media will merge with your environment. A walk will become an adventure through AR. In the area of *health*, a lot will also change—hopefully for the better. Implants will constantly monitor your vital data and provide real-time recommendations on nutrition, exercise, or stress management.

On the way to a future without smartphones, there are also some challenges to overcome. One of these is the issue of *data protection*. Integration into the body or environment makes protection against misuse even more important. The immense amounts of data generated by sensors for monitoring and analysis must also protect privacy. Another key aspect is *cost*. How can these technologies be offered at low cost? And how can these technologies be made *accessible* to the general population? And just as we are already experiencing resistance to the use of AI, since many people primarily want to avoid the dangers of AI, the *technological acceptance* of integrated assistance systems and devices will also be a major hurdle. Not everyone will be immediately willing to accept invasive technologies such as implants.

The world in 15 years will be characterized by seamless integration between humans and technology. Smartphones will be replaced by intelligent, body-worn, and immersive technologies that make life more intuitive, connected, and efficient. But the challenges—from ethics to data protection—will also be part of this exciting future.

It is likely that smartphones will be replaced or supplemented by more advanced and versatile devices in the next ten to fifteen years. A central trend is the development of *smart glasses* and *mixed reality glasses* that seamlessly integrate digital information into our field of vision. With the Vision Pro, Apple has already taken a significant step in this direction. The merging of smart glasses and autonomous vehicles could revolutionize our driving experience. Instead of looking at a central display in the vehicle, information such as navigation, speed, and vehicle status could be projected directly into our field of vision, as with a head-up display. This would not only increase comfort but also improve safety, as your eyes would always remain on the road.

Current Developments by Major Technology Companies

Apple: With the Vision Pro, Apple has introduced an AR/VR headset that offers an immersive experience and projects digital content directly into the field of view. (Computer-Bild, 2024)

Samsung: Samsung is working on its own smart glasses, which are being developed in collaboration with Google. These are expected to offer similar functions to the *Ray-Ban* Meta Smart Glasses and are likely to come to market in 2025. (Inside Digital, 2024)

Google: Google is developing its own AR glasses under the codename "Project Iris," which are intended to look like regular glasses. The release was originally planned for 2024 but has been postponed indefinitely. (Wikipedia, 2024)

5.5 Robot Encounters

Robots have fascinated our author Heiko since his childhood. When a robot independently completes a task, is used in production processes, moves around, and even converses with us, it possesses a certain charm and fascination at the same time. We can interact with a language model via text input or audio, but such an interaction only becomes truly captivating when it takes place with a robot.

Mechanical automatons, such as theater machines with pulleys and steam power, were already conceived by the ancient Greeks (Heron of Alexandria, ca. 300 BC). In the Middle Ages, Leonardo da Vinci tinkered with mechanical knights. True robots in the modern sense have existed since the 1950s, and have been in mass production (at General Motors) since 1961. Until recently, they were mostly known as programmed machines performing specific tasks. This has changed in recent years. Robots can now communicate well, recognize emotions, and execute voice commands.

5.5.1 The Entertainment Robot Pepper

Robots have been around for quite some time. SoftBank Robotics from Japan launched the robot *Pepper* as early as 2014, which quickly gained widespread recognition, especially for its ability to detect and analyze emotions. Pepper also has special capabilities in speech comprehension and output, gesture recognition and nonverbal communication, autonomous movement and navigation, as well as internet access for information retrieval.

Our author Heiko has encountered the robot Pepper several times, whether at trade fairs and conferences, in large department stores, or as shown in this picture (Fig. 5.1), which was taken at an alumni event of

Fig. 5.1 Heiko with robot Pepper

the St. Gallen Management Institute (SGMI) on November 8, 2018 at Deloitte in Berlin.

Sources and further information:

- https://www.softbankrobotics.com
- Learning process: "ball in a cup" (2016) https://youtu.be/jkaRO8J_1XI?si=eACiTzGUH5I53WcS
- Pepper's ChatGPT Integration (2024) https://youtu.be/SsQGAtEuhY0?si=QSj8PgOtzLQZtarD

5.5.2 The Technical Robot Dog Spot

At the COBOTS4YOU trade fair on October 24, 2023 at the Vogel Convention Center in Würzburg, Heiko had the opportunity to see and experience the robot dog *Spot* from *Boston Dynamics* in action (Fig. 5.2).

Fig. 5.2 Heiko with robot Spot

For a moving impression of Spot and other robot developments (such as the famous humanoid robot HD Atlas) from Boston Dynamics, we recommend two very inspiring YouTube videos from Boston Dynamics:

- What does it take to put Spot to work? (2023) https://youtu.be/_Ux-N-NK2GM?si=g8KShWpnDxElLK4y
- Humanoid robot HD Atlas completes fitness course (2024) https://youtu.be/-9EM5_VFlt8?si=fcX-VfHkjMhUQobs

5.5.3 The Humanoid Do-It-Yourself Robot pib

At the Computer Science Festival 2024, the conference of the Gesellschaft für Informatik e. V., on September 24, 2024, Heiko met the humanoid robot pib (and Dr. Jürgen Baier, Managing Director of isento GmbH) (Fig. 5.3).

Pib stands for "*printable intelligent bot*" and is available as a kit for 3D printers. The programs and software are available as open source, making it ideal for printing, building, and programming your own robot at school. Pib is very successful in Germany and has won the ***Digicon Award 2023*** (Munich Digital Innovation Award), the ***CIVIC Innovation Award 2023***, and the ***German Design Award 2025***. Various schools have also won the following prizes with pib:

- P-Seminar Prize Gymnasium Ernestinum in Coburg 2024
- P-Seminar Prize Hans-Sachs-Gymnasium Nuremberg 2024
- Jugend forscht Prize "Human machine interaction" 2024 for Liebfrauen-Schule Bensheim

Pib is very well suited for a seminar, a working group, or a project week at school. The body is completely printed using a 3D printer, then assembled with a kit of hinges and motors. The display and Raspberry Pi can, for example, be connected to ChatGPT via an API interface,

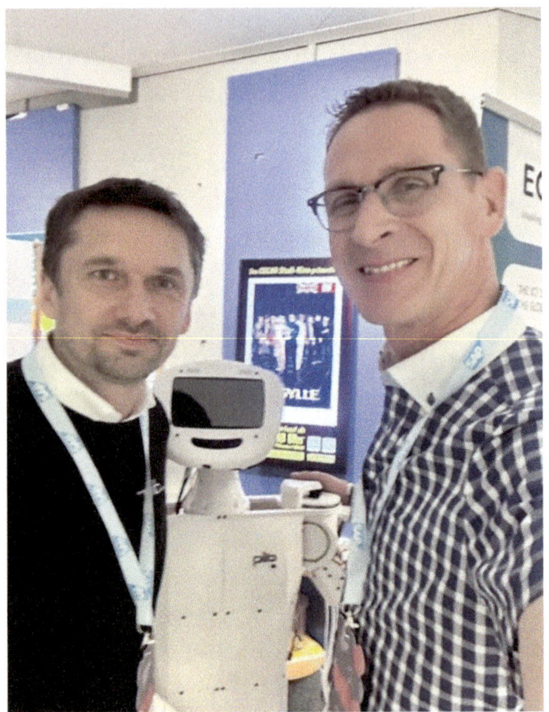

Fig. 5.3 Heiko with robot pib

and just like that, a new classmate is born. The costs are quite moderate and can be financed through the school's support association or a sponsor.

Sources and further information:

- https://pib.rocks

Part III
Symbolic AI

6

Decision Trees as Tools

Contents

In a world full of data, smart decisions are the key to success. But how does a machine make meaningful decisions? While neural networks are often considered a "black box," *decision trees* provide transparent, comprehensible answers. They break down complex problems into simple if-then rules—a cornerstone of *symbolic AI*.

Whether in medicine for diagnosis, in the financial sector for risk analysis, or in manufacturing for quality control—decision trees help extract patterns from structured data and derive well-founded decisions. This chapter explains how decision trees work, where their strengths and

H. Knödel and D. Seipel, *AI and Bots in Everyday Life*,
https://doi.org/10.1007/978-3-658-51144-9_6

limitations lie, and why they continue to play a central role in AI to this day. To make things easier for the reader, this chapter also illustrates the principle of decision trees using a simple example. And to understand the rationale and usefulness of decision trees in AI, we begin by explaining the decision-making process of our human brain and subconscious.

6.1 The Decision-Making Process in Humans

A person makes more than 60,000 decisions every day. Most of these occur unconsciously—estimates suggest that up to 95% of all decisions are controlled by the *subconscious*. Only about 5% of decisions are conscious, meaning those in which we actively think and weigh options.

Automatic processes: Many decisions involve habits, routines, and everyday actions, such as brushing teeth, blinking, or reaching for the phone.

Brain efficiency: The brain uses unconscious patterns and beliefs to save energy and enable quick decisions.

Emotional control: The limbic system, our "emotional brain," evaluates situations in a split second based on experiences and emotions.

Heuristics: Our brain applies simplified thinking strategies to react quickly in complex situations. We are often not even aware of this, as many examples of optical illusions show, where we are deceived into perceiving something different from what is actually there.

In Fig. 6.1 we see an optical illusion. The *Hering illusion* is a geometric-optical illusion developed in 1861 by the German physiologist, brain and perception researcher Ewald Hering (1834–1918) (Hering illusion, 2023). Two straight, parallel lines appear as if they are bowed outward. This is caused by the background pattern of radial lines. The denser the bundle of straight lines, the more intense the illusion effect becomes.

Figure 6.2 shows the so-called Zöllner illusion, which was published in 1860 by the astrophysicist Karl Friedrich Zöllner (1834–1882) and named after him (Zöllner illusion, 2021). Several lines, which are arranged completely parallel to each other, here appear as if they are slanted or converging. This is caused by the short diagonal strokes that cross them.

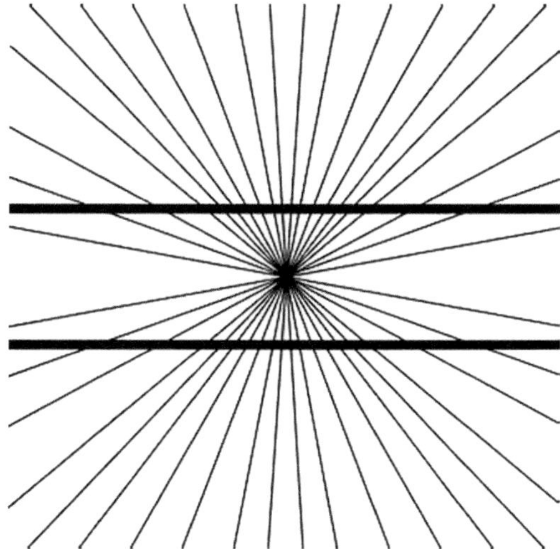

Fig. 6.1 Optical illusion: (Hering illusion, 2023)

Fig. 6.2 Optical illusion: (Zöllner illusion, 2021)

Only about 5% of our decisions are made *consciously*. These include *analytical considerations*: These require cognitive resources, such as when planning, problem-solving, or strategic thinking. The prefrontal cortex, which is responsible for conscious decisions, works significantly slower than the unconscious system.

This raises the question why our subconscious makes so many decisions beyond that. This is largely due to decisions arising from movement processes and reactions.

- *Energy management*: The conscious mind is energy-intensive and cannot handle all tasks alone.
- *Behavioral patterns*: Repeated actions are stored and automated in the brain to free up conscious capacity for new things.
- *Survival mechanism*: Unconscious decisions ensure our survival by enabling quick reactions to potential dangers.

To understand this more precisely, let us briefly look at the role of beliefs. *Beliefs* are deeply rooted convictions in the subconscious that unconsciously influence decisions. They determine how we perceive, evaluate, and react to situations. We often act unconsciously according to these beliefs, for example: "I am not good enough" or "I can do this."

The interplay of *conscious* and *unconscious processes* shows how strongly our lives are influenced by the subconscious. Conscious reflection and "*reprogramming*" of beliefs (NLP, Neuro-Linguistic Programming) can positively change this influence.

6.2 Example of Decision Trees Using a Robotic Sheepdog

Look at the picture. Consider a scenario in which a shepherd, let's call him Otto, uses an AI-powered robotic dog named Robi. Since his sheepdog has grown old and weak, Robi helps him herd the sheep. For this, our AI dog must be able to distinguish between the sheep, the dog, many chickens, and the shepherd himself in order to act accordingly (Fig. 6.3).

Fig. 6.3 Shepherd with his flock, chickens, and sheepdog

Note: The real world is much more complex, with trees, fences, etc., but we want to keep the example as clear as possible. However, you can surely imagine what a robot or robotic dog actually has to accomplish nowadays to move safely through our complex landscape.

Robi uses a decision tree to identify, based on observations, who or what he is dealing with.

Step 1: Definition of features. To build the decision tree, we first define the features that will be used for differentiation:

- *Color* (white, brown, multicolored, none)
- *Size* (small, medium, large)
- *Sounds* (bleating, barking, clucking, speaking, silence)
- *Activity* (walking around, running, hopping, flying, standing still)
- *Number of legs* (2, 3, 4)

Step 2: Building the decision tree. We start with the question that helps us make the first major distinction. Let's assume Robi begins with the feature *color.* That might work right away. In our naive shepherd scene, sheep are *white,* the dog is *black,* the chickens are *brown,* and the shepherd is *blue* (blue jeans) or *multicolored.* But wait: there are also black sheep. – And there are white chickens, brown dogs, shepherds with brown or black clothing. So, the feature color alone is not enough to distinguish between the actors (Fig. 6.4).

Step 3: Branching (further branches). Next, let's add the feature *size.*

- *Multicolored* in combination with *large* leads directly to "shepherd"
- *Multicolored* in combination with *small* leads directly to "chicken"
- *Black* in combination with *large* leads directly to "shepherd"
- *Black* or *white* in combination with *small* leads to another question, which we want to answer using the feature *sounds (noises).*

Step 4: Further branching. So, let's take the next feature, *sounds* (noises).

- For *black* or *white* in combination with *medium,* it could be a dog or a (small) sheep. If Robi hears *barking,* he recognizes a dog; if he hears *bleating,* he recognizes a sheep

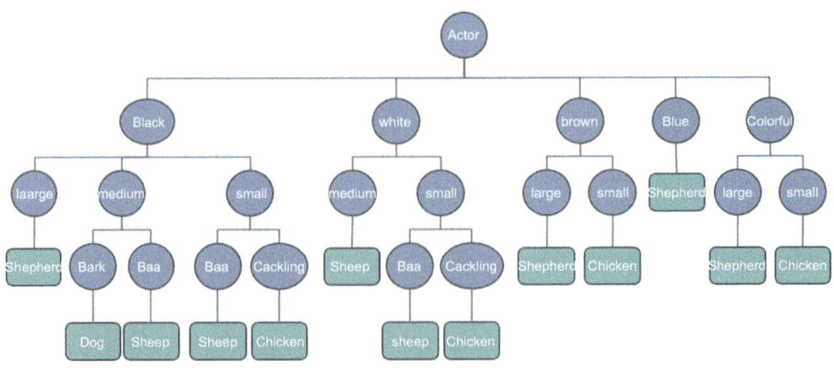

Fig. 6.4 Decision tree for the AI robotic dog Robi

- *Black* or *white* in combination with *small* could be a chicken or a (small) sheep. If Robi hears *bleating*, he recognizes a sheep; if he hears clucking, he recognizes a chicken

And so on and so forth. The more possibilities there are, the larger and more complex the decision tree becomes. You can also add safety checks, such as the shape of the head. Then Robi can distinguish the shepherd from a chicken, even if the shepherd is fooling around and clucking like a chicken.

Step 5: Robi makes decisions. Depending on which features Robi observes, he navigates through this decision tree to identify which animal or the shepherd he is dealing with. Here is a simple example of how Robi would proceed:

- Robi detects *blue* and assumes he is dealing with the shepherd.
- Robi detects *white* and *medium-sized* and assumes he is dealing with a sheep.
- Robi detects *black, small* and hears *bleating. Then* he assumes there is a sheep in front of him.

6.3 Optimization

It is now obvious to consider optimizing such a decision tree so that Robi can make decisions as quickly as possible. For this purpose, the height of the tree and the distribution among the leaves are weighted and evaluated. The tree is then restructured accordingly. In the previous example, it is clear that an initial distinction based on *size* followed by the feature *sounds/noises* leads to faster decisions (Fig. 6.5).

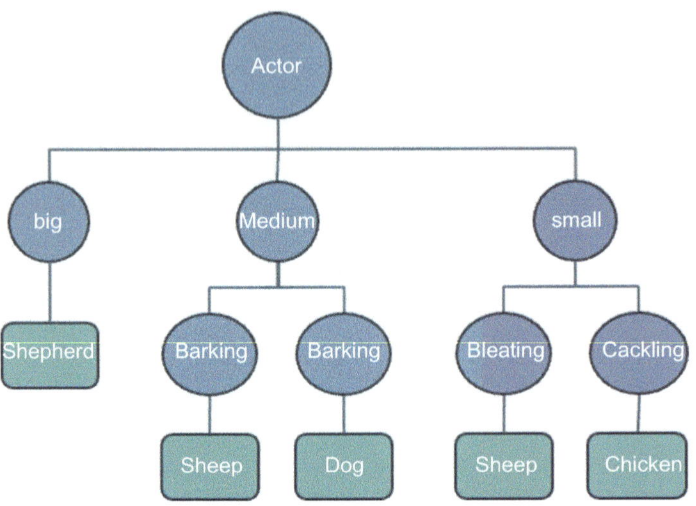

Fig. 6.5 Fast decision paths with an optimal decision tree

6.4 Technical Terms and Explanation

A *decision tree* (German "*Entscheidungsbaum*") always begins with a *root* ("*Wurzel*"). This is the starting point. Fun fact: In computer science, the tree is usually depicted upside down, i.e., the root is at the top and its leaves are at the bottom. The branches, each representing a question or decision criterion, are called *edges* ("*Kanten*"). At the end of each edge, there is either a *node* ("*Knoten*"), which represents the result of an intermediate decision, or a *leaf* ("*Blatt*"), which represents a final outcome. You can also examine *sub trees* ("*Teilbäume*") or branches to break down complex problems ("*Splitting*"). Other common terms, especially in the context of optimizing decision trees, are *entropy* ("*Entropie*"), which measures the impurity of the data, and *information gain* ("*Informationsgewinn*"). An attribute with high information gain significantly reduces the entropy of the dataset and enables a clearer assignment. The nodes are evaluated according to their information content, which allows the decision tree to be optimized. This usually results in a new decision tree that is structured to reach a good decision as quickly as possible by making distinctions at the right points.

6.5 Summary

By using a decision tree, Robi, the AI-powered robotic dog, can effectively distinguish between sheep, another dog, chickens, and the shepherd. Each time Robi encounters an animal or the shepherd, he evaluates the defined features and follows the branches of the decision tree to reach a conclusion. This enables Robi to perform specific tasks, such as herding the sheep, without disturbing the shepherd or the chickens.

Popularity of Decision Trees

Imagine you are trapped in a huge maze, and at every intersection you have to make a decision: left, right, or straight ahead? How do you find your way out? This is exactly where decision trees come into play—not just in real mazes, but in all kinds of problem-solving scenarios in artificial intelligence.

Decision trees are a machine learning method used for classification and regression tasks. They help computers make complex decisions by breaking down a problem into a series of yes/no questions, similar to the branches of a tree. Starting at the root of the tree, each decision follows a branch that leads to further questions until a final decision or prediction is made.

But why are decision trees so popular? Simply put: They are easy to *understand* and *interpret*. Imagine you have data from various weather stations about the current weather and want to decide whether to take an umbrella. A decision tree might start at the root with: "Will it rain?" On its decision path, it encounters questions like "Where is it currently raining?", "Where is the air pressure dropping?", "When will the rain front reach us?" and "Will it still be strong enough then?" Based on the results in the leaves of the decision tree, I can then decide whether to take an umbrella or not. An even simpler question would be "Is it currently raining here?" If yes, you take an umbrella; if not, you don't. The simplicity of decision trees makes them a powerful tool in AI.

Decision trees are also extremely *versatile*. They can be used for almost any type of data and are capable of processing both numerical and categorical data. Whether in finance to assess credit risk, in medicine to make diagnoses, or in retail to predict customer behavior—decision trees provide clear insights and solutions.

Another advantage of decision trees is their ability to handle *large amounts of data* while identifying important variables and ignoring irrelevant ones. This makes them an invaluable tool in today's data-driven world, where the ability to make quick and accurate decisions is crucial.

However, decision trees also have their *limitations*. Without careful constraints, they can become too complex and overly specific to the training data, for example by identifying irrelevant patterns and incorporating them into the decision—a phenomenon known as "overfitting." This can impair the ability of decision trees to make accurate predictions for new, unknown data. Fortunately, there are techniques such as "pruning" the tree that help mitigate this problem.

In summary, decision trees are very important in artificial intelligence. Thanks to their simplicity, versatility, and effectiveness, they enable machines to learn from data and make informed decisions. As with any tool, it is important to use them responsibly and thoughtfully.

7
AI for Knowledge Extraction

Contents

Knowledge Extraction (KE) refers to the process of extracting and structuring knowledge from unstructured data sources such as texts, images, audio, and videos. This process utilizes methods from artificial intelligence (AI), particularly natural language processing (NLP) and machine learning (ML), to identify relevant information and systematically organize it. The following section provides a more detailed explanation of the application of Knowledge Extraction to illustrate its significance and benefits in various contexts.

For those who wish to delve deeper into the subject, or plan to use AI for targeted analysis purposes—such as text, image, or video analysis, or for supporting compliance, risk management, customer support, and personnel in their company—this chapter is dedicated to the technical details and possibilities.

H. Knödel and D. Seipel, *AI and Bots in Everyday Life*,
https://doi.org/10.1007/978-3-658-51144-9_7

This chapter examines the application of advanced concepts such as deep learning, neural network architectures, and the possibilities as well as challenges in data processing. Subsequently, we present a scientific approach to prompt engineering based on Prolog.

7.1 Introduction to Knowledge Extraction with AI

Knowledge Extraction (KE) refers to the process of extracting structured information from unstructured data sources such as texts, images, audio, and video. In this process, unstructured information is transformed into structured information using AI.

AI-powered knowledge extraction technologies use machine learning (ML) and natural language processing (NLP) to identify, extract, and organize relevant information.

The following sections outline key aspects and applications of KE with AI:

7.1.1 Natural Language Processing (NLP)

One of the central techniques of knowledge extraction is natural language processing. NLP enables the analysis and understanding of human language in order to extract relevant information. A typical example of NLP in knowledge extraction is *Named Entity Recognition (NER)*, which identifies entities such as names of people, places, organizations, and dates in texts. Here, information in the text is specifically sought that contains, describes, or is related to this data, such as a person's address or date of birth.

Relation Extraction goes a step further by recognizing and extracting the relationships between these entities and, ideally, also identifying the type of relationship involved. These techniques are particularly useful in large text collections such as scientific articles, news reports, or corporate documents, where they help to extract important information quickly and accurately.

The term *Information Retrieval* refers to searching and retrieving relevant information from large volumes of text. When we humans read a text, we usually remember only about 10 to 15%. That is not a problem, because the rest is irrelevant. This insight is, for example, used in speed reading. And you can think of information retrieval in a similar way. Here, the focus is on searching for main nouns, descriptive adjectives, and, less frequently—depending on requirements—also verbs in the expression. With these, context and relationships can usually be sufficiently described or structured and presented for further processing.

7.1.2 Text Mining and Data Extraction

Text mining refers to the analysis of large volumes of text to identify patterns and extract information. This involves analyzing frequencies, determining and evaluating correlations, and also structuring information.

Pattern matching, for example, searches for identical text components and patterns within a large text. It is also used to standardize texts. In one case study from the banking sector, it was about harmonizing terms, meaning standardizing them as much as possible. During the analysis (at that time without AI assistance), the team came across the term “Kreditanstalt für Wiederaufbau,” which they found multiple times in different forms such as “KfW,” “K.f.W.,” “KFW,” or “Kred. f. Wiederaufbau.” In school, we learn to avoid repetition. This makes sense in prose texts like letters and novels. However, in structured, technical texts and databases, harmonizing terms is very sensible and useful.

An application example where AI evaluates a statement or sentiment in texts, for example in a customer review on social media, is called *sentiment analysis* .We can also simply describe this as “reading between the lines.”

In *topic extraction*, the goal is to identify the main topics and trends in text documents.

By building *knowledge graphs*, entities and their relationships are represented in a structured format.

7.1.3 Automatic Consolidation

Another important application area of knowledge extraction is automatic text summarization (consolidation). Here, long documents are reduced to their essential content, enabling users to grasp the most important information at a glance. This is especially useful in fields such as journalism, where the goal is to turn lengthy articles into short, concise summaries, or in science, where research papers can be reviewed more efficiently.

Summaries can be generated by machine learning models that identify the most important sentences and paragraphs of a text and present them in a logical order. In this process, long texts are automatically shortened with the help of AI methods, text patterns are extracted, or text modules are generated.

Two main types can be distinguished, document summarization and news summarization. In *document summarization*, technical documents, scientific articles, product manuals, business reports, balance sheets, or legal documents are summarized.

In *news summarization*, the primary focus is on the compact presentation of the most important news events, such as in *Tagesschau in 100 s*, where the classic reporting of the day's most important events is reduced from 15 minutes to less than 2 minutes. (ARD Tagesschau, tagesschau in 100 s, 2025).

7.1.4 Image and Video Analysis

In addition to text processing, the analysis of visual data also plays an important role in knowledge extraction. AI-based methods such as object recognition identify and classify objects in images and videos. This is used, for example, in industrial manufacturing for quality control or in security monitoring to detect unwanted events. Another application is optical character recognition (OCR), which detects and extracts text in images. This technique is often used in document digitization to convert printed text into machine-readable form.

A simple example with images is object recognition when searching for dogs or cats in a large number of photos, as most photo apps already offer. Here, outlines and distinctive features of the animals—and, for example, also in facial recognition—are used to find all images with these features. You may have already tried this and noticed that some photos are selected that do not meet the search criteria, and some photos you have in mind are missing from the selection. This illustrates how complex the application of AI methods in *object recognition* is.

Recognition in videos is even more difficult than in images. Here, the pattern or feature changes with every movement in the image. Recognizing a person from the front, from behind, or from the side are different things that need to be combined here.

In *text-in-image recognition* (OCR), text is extracted from an image. *OCR* (*Optical Character Recognition*) is used, for example, to recognize text in photos. When scanning documents such as invoices, insurance documents, and descriptions, especially with old scans, the OCR function is often not activated, so post-processing of the scan is necessary, even if the document was saved in PDF format, because in old PDF formats, images are stored entirely as photos and not broken down into individual objects, as is now automatically done in the latest versions of scanning programs or when using Adobe Acrobat Pro.

Another frequently used method in the context of knowledge extraction and AI is *video summarization*. Just like with document or news summarization, video content is presented as summaries by identifying important scenes and events. Examples include trailers on well-known online streaming TV services, which automatically show a selected scene from a film as a trailer if there is no cinema trailer available for the film. This is often the case with older films—and, to be honest, the quality of the selection here still has significant room for improvement.

7.2 Applications and Benefits for Companies

Due to increasingly affordable data storage capacities and the use of cloud services, we are experiencing a flood of data and information that now seems unmanageable and almost impossible to handle. Everything is being stored, yet we gain little insight from the stored knowledge and experiences. Knowledge extraction is therefore being applied more and more in a wide variety of fields.

7.2.1 Knowledge Management

In *knowledge management*, it helps to systematically capture and make accessible the existing knowledge within a company. By applying knowledge management, knowledge is organized and structured in companies to facilitate access to relevant information, use compact knowledge for analyses, and pass it on to new employees.

7.2.2 Compliance and Risk Management

In the context of *compliance and risk management*, KE supports the automated review and extraction of relevant information from contracts and regulatory documents. This allows compliance rules to be used more quickly and efficiently, for example in detecting money laundering in the banking sector or anonymizing test data in projects. Regulatory requirements can also be implemented more efficiently, and risk assessments can be carried out more comprehensively and with the inclusion of real data.

7.2.3 Customer Service and Support

Another major area of application for KE in companies is its use in *customer service and support*. By automatically extracting information from customer inquiries, these can be processed more efficiently. In most cases, the AI already provides the customer service representative or support staff with relevant answers, allowing them to select the best response. Nowadays, chatbots on the customer support pages of many providers are increasingly capable of answering the majority of customer questions fully automatically, without any human intervention. Only when the AI bot is unable to help further or the customer is dissatisfied with the answer is the conversation forwarded to a "real" support employee.

Knowledge extraction with AI is a powerful tool that enables large amounts of unstructured data to be processed efficiently and transformed into useful, structured information. This offers significant advantages in areas such as knowledge management, compliance, customer service, and more. By integrating NLP (Natural Language Processing), machine learning, and other advanced techniques, companies can gain valuable insights and optimize their processes. The diverse applications of knowledge extraction, from text summarization and image analysis to information retrieval, make it an indispensable tool in modern data processing.

7.2.4 Knowledge Extraction with Prolog

Prolog is a programming language from the family of logic programming languages. It is particularly well-suited for applications in knowledge extraction. This capability is based on its native support for symbolic inference and rule-based application. Knowledge extraction with Prolog leverages these strengths to extract and organize structured information from unstructured data sources. Further information on logic programming in Prolog and DATALOG can be found in an illustrative example in Chap. 8.

Sources and Further Information:
To learn more about knowledge extraction with AI, the following books and scientific papers may be helpful:

Books
- "Natural Language Processing with Python" by Steven Bird, Ewan Klein, and Edward Loper
- Description: This book provides a comprehensive introduction to natural language processing (NLP) techniques with Python. It covers fundamentals such as tokenization, parsing, and named entity

recognition (NER), which are relevant for knowledge extraction. (Bird, 2009)

- "Text Mining and Analysis: Practical Methods, Examples, and Case Studies Using SAS" by Gordon S. Linoff
- Description: This book focuses on text mining and analysis, including techniques for knowledge extraction. It offers practical methods and case studies based on real data. (Linoff, 1997)
- "Mining Text Data" by Charu C. Aggarwal and ChengXiang Zhai
- Description: This book provides a comprehensive overview of text mining techniques, including algorithms and applications for information extraction and text classification. (Aggarwal, 2012)

Scientific Papers

- "Knowledge Extraction and Modeling in a Big Data Context" by Matthias Jarke et al.
  Description: This paper discusses the challenges and techniques of knowledge extraction in the context of large data volumes, including the application of machine learning and NLP. (Jarke et al., 2013)
- "Automatic Extraction of Knowledge from Text: A Survey of Current Techniques and Applications" by Pedro Domingos
  Description: This survey provides an overview of current techniques and applications of automatic knowledge extraction from texts, including NER, relation extraction, and ontology creation. (Domingos)
- "Deep Learning for Natural Language Processing" by Jason Brownlee
  Description: This paper provides an in-depth look at the application of deep learning techniques for NLP tasks, including knowledge extraction. (Brownlee, 2017)

Online Sources

- Coursera course: "Natural Language Processing"
  Description: A comprehensive online course offered by top universities covering the basics and advanced techniques of NLP, including knowledge extraction. (Coursera, 2023)

- Article on Towards Data Science
  Description: "Introduction to Named Entity Recognition" and other articles on this platform provide practical insights and application examples for knowledge extraction. (Towards Data Science, 2020)

8 Knowledge-Based Systems and Logic Programming

Contents

This chapter addresses the role of knowledge-based systems in Artificial Intelligence (AI). Knowledge-based systems play a central role in AI and are among the oldest and most important approaches in this field. Their main function is to represent explicitly encoded knowledge and provide it for problem solving, decision making, or inference.

Logic programming, in turn, plays an important role for knowledge-based systems in AI, as it provides a formal framework for reasoning and problem solving based on formal logic. It offers a declarative programming style, where the "what" (the goals to be achieved) is emphasized instead of the "how" (the concrete evaluation process). In this section, we will explore two practical application examples: the computation of ancestors from a parent relation as a standard example

H. Knödel and D. Seipel, *AI and Bots in Everyday Life*,
https://doi.org/10.1007/978-3-658-51144-9_8

for logic programming, and medical diagnosis of blood types using disjunctive logic programming.

Below, some code snippets in the logic programming languages Prolog and Datalog are listed in blue. Datalog is always printed in italics, Prolog in regular font.

8.1 Knowledge-Based Systems

Knowledge-based systems play a central role in AI and are among the oldest and most important approaches in this field. They can represent explicit knowledge and draw inferences from it to find solutions to problems and make decisions. At the international KRR (Knowledge Representation and Reasoning) conference, important theoretical and practical results are presented annually. They provide a strong foundation for many AI applications where structured knowledge, explanation of decisions, and logical reasoning are required, and they are increasingly used in combination with other approaches such as machine learning.

Knowledge-based systems make it possible to represent expert knowledge in a structured and formal way, for example in the form of rules, facts, ontologies, or semantic networks. They can derive new insights from existing information through inference, in order to make decisions or predictions. Examples include expert systems that provide medical diagnoses based on symptoms and diseases, or systems for technical troubleshooting.

A major advantage of knowledge-based systems is their ability to provide explanations for decisions. Since they are based on explicit rules or data, they can transparently show why a particular conclusion was reached. In contrast to some modern "black box" approaches of machine learning such as neural networks, they are especially useful when traceability is important, for example in medicine and law. Knowledge-based systems can be relatively easily extended and updated. Domain experts can add new knowledge without having to reprogram the system from scratch, since the knowledge is explicitly encoded.

Knowledge-based systems also play a role in *natural language processing (NLP)* and for dialog systems. By using ontologies and semantic networks, a system can better understand how words and concepts are related. In modern AI applications, knowledge-based systems are often combined with machine learning. Such hybrid approaches make it possible to leverage the strengths of both: the symbolic processing of knowledge by knowledge-based systems and the ability to learn from large amounts of data (sub-symbolic).

8.2 Logic Programming

Logic plays an important role in AI, as it provides a formal framework for reasoning and problem solving. It is based on mathematical logics, in particular propositional and predicate logic, and more recently on non-classical logics such as non-monotonic and probabilistic logics, or fuzzy logic. It offers a declarative perspective, where the "what" (i.e., the goals to be achieved) is emphasized instead of the "how" (i.e., the concrete evaluation process). This allows knowledge to be represented precisely and automatic reasoning as well as formal verification to be performed, which is particularly advantageous in symbolic AI applications.

First, we would like to address the notation of facts and rules in Prolog and Datalog, before subsequently elaborating on scientific details and examples.

Notation of Facts and Rules in Prolog and Datalog

The programming languages Prolog and Datalog are logic programming languages based on declarative programming and are particularly used in knowledge representation and logical inference. Both languages use a similar syntax to define facts and rules, but differ in their objectives and application domains.

Facts in Prolog and Datalog
Facts are used in both languages to represent basic knowledge. A fact describes an atomic statement that is either true or false. The syntax of a fact is similar in both languages.

In **Prolog**, facts are written in the form "predicate(argument1, argument2, ...)".

Examples:

parent(maria, anna).
parent(anna, peter).

This states that Maria is a parent of Anna and Anna is a parent of Peter.

The syntax in **Datalog** is almost identical. Facts are also written in the form "predicate(argument1, argument2, ...)":

parent(maria, anna).
parent(anna, peter).

One difference is that Datalog does not provide functionality for more complex data structures, but is limited to relational data.

Rules in Prolog and Datalog
Rules define logical relationships between facts and enable the derivation of new information. A rule consists of a head and a body. The body is a condition that must be satisfied for the head to be considered true.

In **Prolog**, rules are written in the form "Head:- Body", where the head is the fact to be derived and the body represents a condition. Example:

grandparent(X, Y):- parent(X, Z), parent(Z, Y).

This rule states that X is a grandparent of Y if X is a parent of Z and Z is a parent of Y.

The notation of rules in **Datalog** is similar, but does not use function calls or complex data structures. Rules have the form "*Head* ← *Body*" and can look as follows:

grandparent(X, Y)← parent(X, Z) ∧parent(Z, Y).

A key difference is that Datalog works only with positive logical statements and does not support negation or complex control structures like Prolog.

Differences between Prolog and Datalog
Although the syntax of both languages is similar, there are significant differences. Prolog is a general-purpose logic programming language and is suitable for a wide range of applications, including artificial intelligence, rule-based systems, and natural language processing. In contrast, Datalog is more specialized and is mainly used for deductive database applications and queries. Another difference lies in the handling of negation: Prolog supports negation through the technique of negation as failure, while Datalog generally does not support negation or only allows very restricted forms of it, in order to keep computations safe and terminating. Prolog also allows the use of complex data structures such as lists and dynamic terms, whereas Datalog is strictly limited to relational data models.

Formal Representation of Knowledge
Logical expressions can describe facts and relationships between objects, and they make it possible to represent knowledge in a structured and formally correct way; this allows knowledge bases to be built incrementally. For example, facts such as

```
parent(a, b) and parent(b, c)
```

as well as generic rules such as

```
ancestor(X, Y) ← parent(X, Y)
```

express that person a is a parent of b, and that for arbitrary persons, a parent X of Y is also an ancestor. In the logic programming language Prolog, the constants a, b, and c are concrete persons (starting with a lowercase letter), and the variables X and Y (starting with an uppercase letter) can stand for arbitrary values. These syntactic conventions make it possible to dispense with type declarations. The predicate symbols *parent* and *ancestor* must also begin with a lowercase letter in Prolog.

Automated Reasoning. Logic is ideally suited for automated reasoning, in which new facts are derived as conclusions from given facts and rules. A logic-based system can answer a question or make a decision from a set of rules and facts by means of a proof chain. This is especially useful in expert systems or problem solvers. In the example above, one could, for instance, derive *ancestor(a, b)* and *ancestor (b, c)*. Proof trees can explain proof chains for derived facts in logic programs. The explanation component from (Güven et al., 2021) can visualize derived facts for non-monotonic logic programs using an automatically generated proof tree.

Precision and Formal Verification. Since logic is based on mathematical principles, it provides a strong foundation for formal verification and correctness. Systems based on logic are verifiable, and their correctness can be mathematically proven. This is a major advantage in safety-critical systems (such as in aviation or the medical field).

Applications in AI

Logic programming is particularly useful in areas where explicit reasoning and the processing of symbolic information are required. It has played a significant role in the following application areas of AI:

- Logic-based expert systems, for example in medicine and engineering, use rules and facts to make complex decisions.
- In automated planning (e.g., robotics), logic is used to sequence actions and achieve a goal.
- In natural language processing (NLP), logic models are used to support language understanding, meaning representation, and semantic analysis.
- Ontologies and the Semantic Web often use logic-based formalisms for knowledge representation to express connections between concepts.

Declarative Languages

Logic programming, which is based on logical syntax and semantics (Ceri et al., 1990, Lloyd, 1987)—for example, Prolog and DATALOG—belongs to the class of declarative languages: similar to the database language SQL, the knowledge engineer does not need to specify the individual steps to solve a problem; instead, the problem is specified abstractly through compact facts and rules in a logical formalism, which are then evaluated using powerful evaluation methods.[1] In logic programming, a problem is described by rules and facts without explicitly specifying how the solution is to be found. This is particularly helpful in AI, as it allows the system to independently find solutions through inference or algorithms. The programmer specifies what is to be achieved, and the system itself decides on the best way to do so. Well-known concepts include forward and backward chaining as well as non-monotonic evaluation methods such as perfect or stable models. In an application domain such as planning (for example, in robotics), the goal can be defined, and the system finds a plan to achieve this goal.

Logic Programming in Prolog and DATALOG

Prolog (Programming in Logic) is the best-known language of logic programming; it has had a major influence on the development of AI. In the context of databases, the DATALOG variant is often used. Prolog is frequently used for applications in AI that deal with symbolic processing, knowledge representation, and automated reasoning.

The following DATALOG rules of the form *head* ← *body* are, for example, often used to describe that *X* is an ancestor of *Y* if *X* is a parent of *Y*, or if *X* is a parent of *Z* and *Z* is an ancestor of *Y*:

```
ancestor(X, Y) ← parent(X, Y).

ancestor(X, Y) ← parent(X, Z) ∧ ancestor(Z, Y).
```

[1] In contrast, most programming languages used today are called imperative or procedural; in addition, current programming languages—such as Java and Python—are, of course, usually also object-oriented.

The second rule is recursive, since *ancestor* also refers to itself. By linking *parent* and *ancestor*, new ancestors can be derived. Syntactically, Prolog and DATALOG differ in that Prolog uses the symbol ":-" instead of the rule arrow " $\leftarrow$ ", and the comma instead of the conjunction $\wedge$. Prolog uses backward chaining (top-down evaluation) to answer queries, while DATALOG derives new knowledge from facts using forward chaining (bottom-up evaluation). In Prolog, the programmer must ensure that recursive derivations terminate, which is not a problem for the *parent* relation in this example. In DATALOG, termination is guaranteed. However, its expressive power is somewhat limited, and all variables in a rule must also appear in the positive body so that forward chaining works.

In practice, logic programming also requires aggregations (known from SQL), default negation, and meta-predicates, which demand sophisticated concepts for evaluating logic programs. In addition, hybrid knowledge sources, for example with complex structured knowledge, often need to be linked. The declarative programming system *Declare* provides concepts for this (Seipel, 2024).

An Example of Knowledge Extraction in Prolog

Prolog is excellently suited for *Knowledge Extraction* due to its ability to perform logical inference and apply rules. It enables the implementation of *Named Entity Recognition*, *Relation Extraction*, and *Text Consolidation* in a declarative manner, making programming more intuitive and comprehensible.

Named Entity Recognition (NER): Identification of people and places in texts.

```
% Facts
entity(john, person).
entity(london, place).
% Rule
extract_entities(Text, Entities):-
    findall(Entity,
            (member(Word, Text), entity(Word, Entity)),
            Entities).
```

```
% Query
?- extract_entities([john, visited, london], Entities).
% Entities = [person, place]
```

In this example, Prolog extracts entities such as 'person' and 'place' from a list of words by checking the predefined facts.

Relation Extraction: Detecting relationships between entities in texts.

```
% Fact
relation(john, visited, london).
% Rule
extract_relations(Text, Relations):-
    findall((Subject, Relation, Object),
                    (member([Subject, Relation, Object], Text),
relation(Subject, Relation, Object)),
Relations).
% Query
?- extract_relations([[john, visited, london]], Relations).
```

Here, a relationship such as 'visited' between 'john' and 'london' is extracted, based on predefined relationships in the facts.

Text Consolidation: Summarizing a text by extracting the most important sentences.

```
% Facts
important_sentence('John visited London.', important).
important_sentence('He met the Queen.', important).
important_sentence('They had tea.', not_important).

% Rule
summarize_text(Text, Summary):-
    findall(Sentence,
                        (member(Sentence, Text), important_sen-
tence(Sentence, important)),
Summary).

% Query
```

```
?- summarize_text(['John visited London.', 'He met the
Queen.', 'They had tea.'], Summary).

% Summary = ['John visited London.', 'He met the Queen.']
```

In this case, Prolog extracts only the important sentences, based on previously defined criteria, thus creating a summary of the text.

8.3 Non-classical Extensions – ASP/DLP

In many practical applications, logic programming must also deal with uncertainty or incomplete knowledge. Non-classical extensions such as non-monotonic and fuzzy logic or probabilistic logics address these limitations (Steen & Benzmüller, 2024). In theory, more sophisticated inference methods are used here, which we cannot describe in detail. Instead, in practice, we rely on the intuitive understanding of declarative facts and rules.

Answer Set Programming (ASP) (Baral, 2010) and *Disjunctive Logic Programming (DLP)* (Lobo et al., 1992), as a special case thereof, are also non-monotonic extensions that can handle incomplete knowledge. We will take a closer look at these. ASP can handle default negations; in DLP, even disjunctive clauses can be used to link several possible alternatives in the conclusions of a rule with OR, whereas in classical logic programming each rule must have exactly one conclusion. In DLP, the logical rules have the following general syntax: $A_1 \vee \ldots \vee A_k \leftarrow B_1 \wedge \ldots \wedge B_m \wedge not\ C_1 \wedge \ldots \wedge\ not\ C_n$. The possible conclusions $A_1, \ldots, A_n$ are thus connected disjunctively. The conditions $B_1, \ldots, B_m$ (positive body) must all be satisfied and the conditions $C_1, \ldots, C_n$ (negative body) must not (conjunction), so that at least one of the conclusions becomes true. *not* denotes default negation.

An Example of Blood Group Diagnosis

A detailed example of blood group diagnosis is used to illustrate DLP.

Each child inherits one *genotype* from each of their two parents. In the following figure, the father (f) has phenotype a with genotypes a

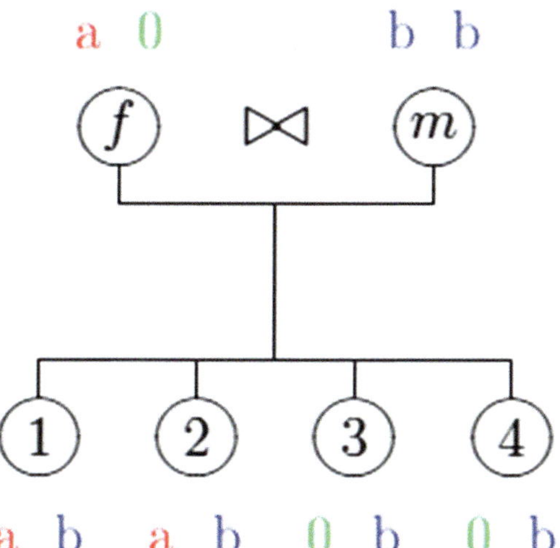

Fig. 8.1 Representation of genotypes for blood group diagnosis

and 0, and the mother (m) has phenotype b with two genotypes b; thus, 2 out of the 4 combinations of the children are identical. The children either have phenotype ab (with the two genotypes a and b) or phenotype b (with the two genotypes 0 and b) (Fig. 8.1).

Depending on the genotype (gt), a person is heterozygous or homozygous:

```
heterozygous (P, T1 , T2) ← gt (P, T1) ∧ gt (P, T2) ∧ diff
(T1 , T2).
heterozygous (P ) ← heterozygous (P, T1 , T2).
homozygous (P, T ) ← gt (P, T ) ∧ not heterozygous (P ).
```

The following disjunctive rule states that a person must have at least one genotype. The subsequent rule "←…" with an empty head ($k=0$) is called an integrity constraint; it states that a person can have at most two different genotypes, since three pairwise different genotypes lead to inconsistency (expressed by the empty head):

```
gt (P, a) ∨ gt (P, b) ∨ gt (P, 0 ) ← person(P ).
← gt (P, T1) ∧ gt (P, T2) ∧ gt (P, T3) ∧ diff (T1 , T2 , T3).
```

With the following rules, one can infer the genotypes of children from the genotypes of their parents:

```
gt (Child, T_1) ∨ gt (Child, T_2) ←
parent (Child, Parent ) ∧ heterozygous (Parent, T_1 , T_2).
gt (Child, T ) ← parent (Child, Parent ) ∧ homozygous (Parent,
T ).
```

The phenotypes (pt: a, b, ab, or 0) of a person depend on their genotypes:

```
pt (P, a) ∨ pt (P, b) ∨ pt (P, ab) ∨ pt (P, 0 ) ← person(P ).
pt (P, X) ← heterozygous (P, X, 0).
pt (P, ab) ← heterozygous (P, a, b).
pt (P, X) ← homozygous (P, X).
```

If the rules shown are combined with the *ancestor* rules from earlier, then diagnoses for ancestors can also be derived. However, the conclusions become weaker (longer disjunctions).

Advantages and Areas of Application

The *advantages* of DLP/ASP are their enhanced expressive power and the ability to model non-determinism:

- Both make it possible to represent complex knowledge structures in which multiple alternatives are possible, without forcing a unique conclusion. This is useful in scenarios involving uncertainty or incomplete knowledge.
- They are therefore particularly well suited for describing non-deterministic problems where multiple possible solutions exist, but it is not clear which one is correct.

The *areas of application* are often in fields where uncertainty plays a role, such as diagnosis, planning, or decision-making.

- In medical or technical diagnostic systems, disjunctive rules can be used to infer several possible causes of a disease from an observed symptom.
- In automated planning, there may be situations where different actions lead to the same goal, and there may be several possible suitable sequences of actions.
- LP is often combined with non-monotonic logics—such as abductive logic—to find alternative explanations (hypotheses) for observed phenomena.

8.4 Hybrid Approaches and Hybrid Knowledge Sources

The state of the art in *neuro-symbolic AI* is summarized in (Hitzler & Sarker, 2021). Five categories are examined: By default, input and output are in symbolic form, but processing is neural. In contrast, *AlphaGo*, *AlphaZero*, and current approaches for autonomous vehicles embed neural pattern recognition into a symbolic problem solver. Conversely, symbolic reasoning can be embedded into a neural machine. In *Deep Learning for Symbolic Mathematics*, symbolic rules are "compiled away" through training. In neuro-symbolic concept learning, there is ultimately a transition from a neural system to symbolic inference. Hybrid AI combines sub-symbolic and symbolic approaches (Battaglia et al., 2018, Goertzel, 2012, McMillan et al., 1992, Smolensky, 1987).

In practice, hybrid knowledge sources must also be handled, e.g., relational, complex, semi-structured data together with knowledge from the *Semantic Web*. The declarative tool *FNQUERY (PL4XML)* (Seipel, WLP, 2002) was, for example, developed in Prolog to enable querying, transforming, and updating XML data together with relational and *Semantic Web data* and *knowledge graphs*.

For example, neural networks (Convolutional Neural Network, CNN) can be used to extract symbolic data (the ball trajectories) from tennis videos, which can then be further processed using declarative methods—rules, grammars—for data mining and symbolic analysis.

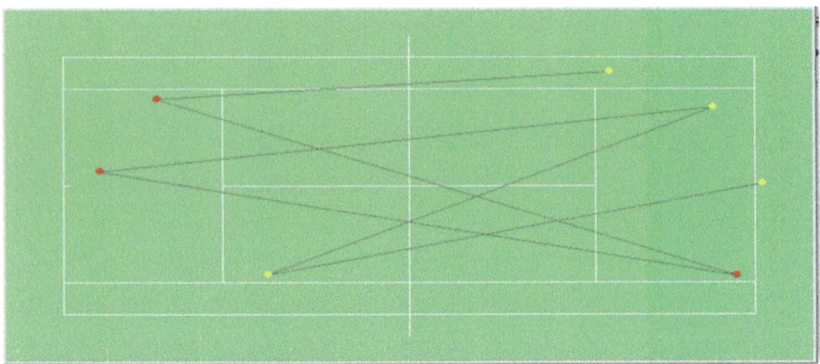

Fig. 8.2 Graphical representation of tennis analysis

The following image shows the extracted impact points of a rally, where after a serve from the right, at the end of the rally, the left player hit a longline shot—along the upper sideline—just out of bounds (Fig. 8.2).

In the tennis tool, it was advantageous to store the extracted rallies in *Extended Markup Language* XML and then analyze them symbolically using Prolog and *FNQUERY*.

Part IV

Trends, Ethics, and the Future of AI

9

Opportunities, Risks, and Ethics of AI

Contents

Finally, we explore the ethical aspects of AI and examine possible future scenarios. How do we handle data protection? What are the societal impacts? This chapter challenges the reader to think beyond the technology itself.

9.1 Opportunities through AI

The deployment and utility of artificial intelligence offers significant advantages, streamlining workflows and enhancing overall quality of life. Below, we outline what we consider to be the most efficient and advanced benefits of AI.

H. Knödel and D. Seipel, *AI and Bots in Everyday Life*,
https://doi.org/10.1007/978-3-658-51144-9_9

Increased economic efficiency: Artificial intelligence is used to automate repetitive tasks, allowing companies to save time and costs. It assists in decision-making by analyzing and processing vast amounts of data, for instance for market analyses or strategic planning. In logistics, AI also optimizes supply chains, routes, and inventory management, making the flow of goods more streamlined.

Advances in medicine: In the medical field, AI enables more precise diagnoses and personalized treatment plans by analyzing medical data and identifying patterns. Systems like IBM Watson support doctors in the early disease detection and in selecting the best therapy. Furthermore, AI accelerates drug development by identifying promising active substances more rapidly.

Education and access to knowledge: AI-based learning platforms personalize the learning process by adapting content to the user's learning pace and needs. Language barriers are overcome through the use of translation and language processing tools, making education more accessible worldwide. Teachers also benefit from the analysis of learning progress, enabling them to address students' specific weaknesses more effectively.

Improved quality of life: Smart home systems with integrated AI make everyday life more convenient by automating and simplifying tasks. People with disabilities benefit from technologies such as speech recognition and text-to-speech systems, which help to break down barriers. In addition, AI offers personalized recommendations to cater to individual preferences in areas like entertainment or shopping. This will also extend to the field of autonomous driving and, more generally, driving comfort, for example upon entering a car, we might be greeted by our favorite podcast, the news, or a playlist tailored to our current mood—which the AI will, of course, have automatically detected as we stepped in.

Environmental and climate protection: AI helps to use energy more efficiently, for example by optimizing energy consumption in buildings and cities. In climate research, environmental data is analyzed and AI supports the prediction of extreme weather events or the development of sustainable solutions. AI also contributes to recycling by efficiently identifying and sorting waste.

Advances in science and research: Data science, predictive analytics, and data mining are fields that have been intensively engaged in data analysis for decades. Thanks to improved computing power and capacity, scientists can now specifically use AI to analyze large datasets more quickly, accelerating breakthroughs in research. It helps in the discovery of new phenomena, such as unknown planets or cosmic anomalies. Furthermore, AI enables precise simulations in physics, chemistry, and biology that can answer complex questions.

Security and crisis management: By analyzing real-time data, AI can detect and respond to natural disasters such as earthquakes or floods at an early stage. In the field of cybersecurity, AI protects systems by detecting and blocking potential attacks. Additionally, AI-controlled drones support disaster relief by delivering aid supplies to hard-to-reach areas.

Improved mobility: Autonomous vehicles controlled by AI can make road traffic safer and more efficient. AI systems can often detect and respond to hazards more quickly, as cameras around the car are vigilant every millisecond. In traffic management, AI optimizes the control of traffic lights and schedules to reduce congestion. AI also enables innovative mobility services, such as flexible ride-sharing options that better accommodate individual needs.

9.2 Dangers of Artificial Intelligence

AI is increasingly integrated into many areas of life—from healthcare and business to entertainment. However, this rapid development also introduces significant dangers that should not be overlooked. The following sections outline key challenges associated with the growing use of AI.

Loss of control: In some areas, AI systems may operate beyond full human interpretability, as they are capable of making independent decisions based on algorithms that humans often can no longer fully comprehend. This "black box" nature carries the risk that we lose control, especially in safety-critical applications such as autonomous vehicles or military drones.

Ethics and discrimination: AI systems are only as objective as the data with which they are trained. Biased or discriminatory training data can lead to unfair decisions, for example in the granting of loans or in recruitment processes. This exacerbates social inequalities and can trigger serious ethical conflicts.

Fake news and disinformation: AI significantly lowers the barrier for *social engineering* attacks. By using LLMs to craft highly convincing, personalized *phishing* emails or using voice cloning for 'CEO fraud,' attackers can manipulate individuals into divulging sensitive corporate information with unprecedented success rates. AI-powered tools can be used to create fake identities to deceive people and steal data—deceptively realistic videos, images, or audio recordings that are deliberately used to spread disinformation. This threatens democracy by undermining trust in media and institutions.

Deepfake videos are a prime example of manipulation and abuse enabled by AI. Fake videos can be used to cause reputational damage, fraud, or political conflict. Although technologies for detecting fake news are also constantly evolving, they often lag behind the latest deepfake techniques. A race similar to that between viruses and anti-virus programs is beginning.

Job loss and social inequality: Automation through AI is increasingly replacing human labor, especially in routine and manufacturing jobs. This can cause mass unemployment and further widen the gap between the winners and losers of digitalization.

Security risks from cyberattacks: AI can be used as both a defensive and offensive tool in cybersecurity. Attackers and hackers could use AI to carry out targeted attacks on infrastructures or systems, while defenders may struggle to keep up with these dynamic threats. It is therefore important to engage with AI early on and to consider countermeasures that may be sensible and useful.

Abusive use of surveillance information: AI-driven surveillance technologies enable complete control of the population. This is most likely to be found in countries with authoritarian regimes. Authoritarian states use AI-powered surveillance systems to curtail civil rights and suppress opposition movements.

Dependence on AI systems: The growing dependence on AI in areas such as healthcare, transportation, or energy supply increases vulnerability to disruptions, failures, and manipulation. A system error can have catastrophic consequences.

Real and Serious Aspects

These dangers are real and serious aspects that accompany the use and further development of AI. The following is an assessment of each point.

Data privacy threats: Many AI systems, especially generative models like ChatGPT, store and analyze inputs to improve the system. If sensitive data is entered, there is a risk that it may be misused or inadvertently reproduced in later interactions.

Power politics: Authoritarian states are making secret, massive investments in AI to gain an advantage or perhaps even dominance. Since these developments are usually not as transparent as in democratic states, this also poses a certain danger, as international cooperation and standards for the development and use of AI with these countries are often impossible or cannot take place on a confidential level. This will intensify geopolitical tensions and trigger an AI arms race. Furthermore, this could shift the focus from ethical development to power politics.

Military use: The use of AI-powered weapons, robots, and drones in the military carries extreme risks, especially with autonomous weapon systems (LAWS)[1]. These could make lethal decisions without human control, raising ethical and security policy concerns. At the same time, terrorists could misuse such technologies.

9.3 Data Protection and Security

Protecting privacy and the security of data in connection with artificial intelligence (AI) is essential to build trust and uphold ethical standards. A central principle is *data minimization*. AI systems should collect only

[1] The abbreviation LAWS stands for Lethal Autonomous Weapon System.

the data that is absolutely necessary for their operation. This approach minimizes the risk of data misuse and ensures that sensitive information is not processed unnecessarily. The extent of data usage depends on the specific application. Many AI simulations and scenarios require large amounts of data (big data) to gain insights that are not obvious or apparent. When processing large volumes of data, it is therefore more important to ensure a secure system environment. For rapid analyses and text-based applications, it is advisable to minimize the amount of data as much as possible and to anonymize it if possible.

In addition, *transparency* plays a crucial role. Users should be clearly informed about what data is being collected, for what purpose, and how this data is used. Open communication not only fosters trust but also helps to avoid misunderstandings or uncertainties in dealing with AI systems.

Another important aspect is the *anonymization* of data. Wherever possible, personal information should be anonymized or at least pseudonymized. This step serves to protect users' privacy and prevent misuse. Especially in a world where data is a central resource, this is an indispensable mechanism for safeguarding individual rights.

Security measures are also of great importance. The protection of stored data must be ensured through the use of modern technologies such as encryption, strict access controls, and regular security audits. These measures help prevent unauthorized access and maintain the integrity of the data.

Finally, the *right to be forgotten* is a central concern in the context of the *General Data Protection Regulation (GDPR)*. Users should always have the option to request the deletion of their data, especially when it is processed by AI systems. This strengthens individuals' control over their own data and ensures that it is not stored or used permanently once it is no longer needed.

By adhering to these principles, data protection and security in the AI environment can be significantly improved. This is not only a legal requirement, but also a prerequisite for upholding ethical standards and fostering long-term trust in AI technologies. Therefore, a core principle is accountability.

9.4 Ethical Considerations and Discussions

The development and use of Artificial Intelligence (AI) brings with it a multitude of ethical issues that are of fundamental importance to society. A central aspect is the assumption of *responsibility*. Developers and users of AI systems must take responsibility for the decisions and actions of AI, especially when these decisions have significant impacts on people. A clear assignment of responsibility is essential to prevent misuse and undesirable developments.

Another key value is *fairness*. AI should be developed in such a way that it does not produce discriminatory or biased outcomes. This requires careful review of the datasets and algorithms used to ensure they are free from distortions and prejudices. Fairness is a fundamental building block for ensuring social justice and equal opportunities in a digitalized world.

Transparency and explainability also play a crucial role. It should be comprehensible how and why an AI arrives at certain decisions. This traceability is important not only for professionals but also for end users, in order to build trust and better understand the use of AI systems.

Another important principle is *harm prevention*. AI systems are expected to be designed to minimize potential harm to people and society. This includes both physical and psychological harm. Developers are obliged to analyze possible risks and develop strategies to minimize them.

Finally, *autonomy and control* of humans is a central concern. Users should always retain control over AI systems and be able to question or revise their decisions. This is indispensable, especially for critical decisions, such as in medicine or the judiciary. The design of AI should always aim to respect and support human autonomy.

By adhering to these ethical principles, it can be ensured that Artificial Intelligence is used responsibly and for the benefit of society. They form the foundation for a sustainable and ethical approach to a technology that has the potential to fundamentally change the world.

9.5 The EU Commission's AI Act

The EU AI Act (AI Law, (European Commission, 2024)) represents one of the most comprehensive regulatory frameworks for artificial intelligence (AI) and aims to govern the handling of AI systems in Europe. Companies and organizations face the challenge of adapting to the new regulations and meeting the associated compliance requirements. In this section, we highlight the key aspects addressed by the AI Act and provide practical recommendations for action.

The entry into force of the AI Act on **August 1, 2024** marked the beginning of a new era of AI regulation in Europe, with the goal of promoting trust, transparency, and accountability in the use of AI technologies. In addition to regulation, the aim is also to foster innovation while minimizing risks and protecting fundamental rights. For small and medium-sized enterprises (SMEs), this means new obligations and adjustments in daily business.

Risk-Based Approach

One of the central features of the AI Act is the *risk-based approach*, which divides AI systems into four categories. This differentiation is intended to address specific risks without hindering innovation. The first category includes **unacceptable risks**, where the use of AI systems is completely prohibited. This includes, for example, applications that could violate fundamental rights, such as AI-based social scoring systems or technologies for covert surveillance. The second category refers to applications with **high risk**, which are subject to strict requirements. These include, for example, AI systems in healthcare, law enforcement, or the judiciary. Companies that develop or operate such systems must prepare extensive documentation, conduct risk assessments, and ensure continuous monitoring.

For applications with **limited risk**, such as chatbots, specific transparency requirements apply. For example, users must be explicitly informed that they are interacting with an AI. The fourth category, which includes most AI applications, covers systems with **minimal risk**, such as game AIs or image editing programs. These applications are not subject to specific regulatory requirements in order to avoid excessive bureaucracy.

Regulation of High-Risk AI

A particular focus of the AI Act is the regulation of high-risk AI systems. These applications, which can directly affect the lives and safety of people, must meet strict requirements. Companies are obliged to ensure that the data used is representative, of high quality, and free from bias. This is essential to avoid discriminatory or erroneous outcomes. In addition, the systems must be designed to be transparent and traceable, so that all decisions made by AI can be documented and, if necessary, explained. Continuous monitoring of such systems and the implementation of risk mitigation mechanisms are also indispensable. The approach known as *Human in the Loop* ensures that a human remains actively involved in decision-making, while the AI system only provides suggestions and decision support. Companies must establish mechanisms that enable humans to intervene in and control the decisions of the AI system. This is intended to prevent automated processes from making critical decisions without sufficient oversight, especially in safety-relevant or ethically sensitive areas. A particularly important component is *human oversight*, i.e., human supervision of AI systems, which—especially for high-risk AI systems (such as medical interventions, applicant selection, or credit approval)—ensures that a human can intervene in the AI system when necessary and shut it down in an emergency.

Transparency Obligations

Another important component of the AI Act is the transparency requirements. Users must be informed when they are interacting with an AI. This applies, for example, to *chatbots*, which must clearly indicate that they are not human contacts. The same applies to so-called *deepfakes*—that is, AI-generated images or videos—which must also be clearly labeled as such. These transparency obligations are intended to ensure that users are not deceived and always know what type of system they are dealing with.

Promotion of Innovation

In addition to regulatory requirements, the AI Act aims to promote innovation. For this purpose, so-called "regulatory sandboxes" have been introduced. These test and simulation environments offer companies the opportunity to develop and test new technologies in a controlled setting. Especially for small and medium-sized enterprises (SMEs), these sandboxes provide valuable support, as they allow for experimentation without being directly subject to comprehensive regulatory requirements. The goal is to facilitate innovation while ensuring that the technologies tested comply with legal requirements before they are brought to market.

Penalties and Enforcement

To ensure compliance with the regulations, the AI Act provides for strict sanctions. Violations of the provisions can be punished with fines of up to 6% of the company's global annual turnover. Examples of violations include the use of prohibited AI systems, failure to comply with transparency obligations, or inadequate monitoring of high-risk applications. These strict penalties are intended to serve as a deterrent and ensure that companies take legal requirements seriously and integrate them into their internal processes.

Sources and Further Information

- **Official Draft of the EU AI Act (2021):** European Commission. "Proposal for a Regulation laying down harmonized rules on Artificial Intelligence (Artificial Intelligence Act)" (European Union, 2025)
- **Explanatory Summary:** European Parliament. "Artificial Intelligence Act: Ensuring AI that is trustworthy and human-centric." (European Parliament, 2025)
- **Report on AI Risk Assessment:** High-Level Expert Group on Artificial Intelligence. "Ethics Guidelines for Trustworthy AI." (European Commission, Ethics Guidelines for Trustworthy AI, 2019)
- **AI in School Education:** "Ethical Guidelines for the Use of Artificial Intelligence (AI) and Data in Education" by the European Union (European Union, Ethical Guidelines for the Use of Artificial Intelligence (AI) and Data in Education, 2025)

The Staggered Implementation Deadlines of the AI Act Are as Follows

February 1, 2025: Ban on AI systems with unacceptable risk.
May 1, 2025: Application of codes of conduct.
August 1, 2025: Rules for General Purpose AI (GPAI) become applicable.
August 1, 2026: Application for most AI systems, including high-risk systems as per Annex III.
August 1, 2027: Full application of the law for all risk categories.

The AI Act follows a risk-based approach, with stricter requirements the higher the risk to health, safety, or fundamental rights. The regulation applies to all providers of AI systems that are used or made accessible in the EU, regardless of the company's location. The aim of the law is to balance the benefits and risks of AI, enabling progress and development while safeguarding the interests of users.

Within the EU Commission, an AI Office will be established to monitor the implementation and compliance with the regulations. For companies, this means new compliance requirements, ranging from adapting existing systems to creating technical documentation. These requirements, especially for SMEs, are associated with financial and organizational effort.

Compliance with the General Data Protection Regulation (GDPR) remains essential and is supplemented by the AI Act in the context of AI. Companies must ensure that their AI systems are data protection compliant and are continuously audited. By adhering to these requirements, responsible use of AI can be promoted and public trust strengthened.

Compliance and Regulation

Compliance with the standards prescribed by the AI Act is indispensable for companies to avoid legal and financial risks. The regulation particularly includes requirements for transparency, risk assessment, and data protection. Companies must ensure that their AI systems comply with the requirements at every stage of the lifecycle, from development and operation to decommissioning.

Building Compliance Staff

The establishment of specialized compliance teams is an essential step in meeting the requirements of the AI Act. Companies should create specialized roles, such as an AI Compliance Officer, who is responsible for overseeing all AI-related activities. Their tasks include conducting audits, training employees, and updating internal policies in line with legal requirements.

In addition, interdisciplinary teams consisting of representatives from IT, legal, human resources, and management can make valuable contributions. These teams should develop strategies for regulatory compliance, manage risks, and maintain dialogue with external regulatory authorities. Building such structures helps ensure ongoing compliance while enabling the smooth integration of legal requirements into business processes.

Adapting to New Regulations

The introduction of the AI Act requires comprehensive adaptation of internal processes and structures. Companies should review and, if necessary, adjust their internal procedures to implement the new regulations. This includes creating a compliance strategy specifically focused on AI systems. A proactive approach can help companies minimize regulatory risks.

Documentation and Transparency

A central aspect of the AI Act is the requirement for comprehensive documentation and transparency. Companies must ensure that their AI systems are traceable and that decisions can be explained transparently. This requires detailed records of data sources, algorithms, and decision-making processes.

Risk Assessment

The risk assessment of AI systems is a key factor in the new regulation. Companies must identify and evaluate the potential risks of their systems and take appropriate risk mitigation measures. The introduction of a risk-based approach can help minimize security issues and increase acceptance of the technologies.

Data Management and Data Protection

Efficient data management and strict data protection are essential components of the AI Act. Companies must ensure that data processing complies with the requirements of the General Data Protection Regulation (GDPR). Topics such as data minimization, purpose limitation, and data security play a central role in this context.

Employee Training

Employee training is a key factor in implementing the requirements of the AI Act. The workforce should be trained in the areas of AI, compliance, and ethical standards. Regular continuing education measures ensure that employees understand the importance of the regulations and are able to apply them in practice.

Importance and Implementation of Employee Training

Training employees plays a central role in ensuring that AI systems are used correctly, monitored, and risks are identified. Targeted training enables companies to ensure compliance with the AI Act while minimizing legal risks.

Necessity of Training

Employees must possess the necessary knowledge to understand the technical, legal, and ethical aspects of AI systems. In particular, operation, monitoring, and risk assessment require specific expertise. Below, we present three examples of departments that will be among the first to use and benefit from AI:

- *Human Resources (HR):*
  The use of AI-based systems in the HR department, especially for applicant selection and employee evaluation, requires a deep understanding of how these technologies work. Training content should focus on explaining AI systems, avoiding potential discrimination, and ensuring compliance with data protection regulations. The goal is for all HR employees to receive comprehensive training in these areas by the end of 2025, in order to successfully implement legal requirements and ensure compliance.

- *Sales Department:*
  The use of AI for customer analysis and sales strategies opens up new opportunities for the sales department to optimize their work. To ensure responsible use of these technologies, training should aim to teach the interpretation of AI-generated data, emphasize the ethical handling of sensitive customer data, and ensure compliance with data protection laws. The goal is for all sales employees to be comprehensively trained by the end of 2025 to ensure the responsible use of AI in sales and to meet compliance requirements.
- *IT Department:*
  The development, implementation, and maintenance of AI systems is the responsibility of the IT department, which plays a central role in implementing the AI Act. To meet this responsibility, training should cover technical aspects of AI, security measures, risk assessments, and the legal requirements of the AI Act. The goal is for IT staff to be given priority and comprehensive training, ideally already during 2025, to ensure compliance with regulatory requirements and to guarantee the smooth implementation of AI systems.

Implementation of a Training Plan

The starting point of an effective training program is the *needs analysis*. Companies must carefully analyze which departments and employees require specific training. This includes identifying roles that work directly with AI systems, such as in the IT department, HR, or sales. Positions that are indirectly affected, such as compliance officers or managers who make decisions based on AI analyses, must also be considered. A comprehensive needs analysis forms the basis for the targeted development of an effective training plan.

Based on the results of the needs analysis, a detailed *training plan* should be developed. This plan should take into account the specific needs of each department and employee group. It is important to tailor the training content to the respective roles and responsibilities of the employees. For example, IT staff should receive in-depth knowledge of technical aspects of AI and risk management, while HR staff require training on ethical and data protection aspects of AI systems. The plan should also define clear timelines and milestones to ensure that training is completed on schedule.

Once the training plan has been developed, the next step is the *implementation of the training*. All relevant employees should complete the planned training within the specified timeframe. Various methods can be used here, such as in-person workshops, e-learning modules, or hybrid training formats. Important topics to be covered include compliance with transparency obligations, the safe handling of AI systems, as well as risk assessment and documentation. The training should not only impart knowledge but also promote the practical application of the content to ensure that employees can effectively apply what they have learned in their daily work.

Given the rapid development of AI technologies and the associated legal frameworks, the *continuous further training* of employees is indispensable. Regular updates and refreshers of training content help ensure that the workforce always remains up to date. Companies should establish continuing education programs that enable employees to stay informed about technological advances, new regulatory requirements, and best practices. Such programs can also help strengthen the organization's capacity for innovation and foster confidence in handling AI systems.

Through systematic training planning and a sustainable culture of continuing education, companies can successfully meet the challenges of the AI Act while establishing a solid foundation for the responsible use of AI.

Certification and Quality Assurance

Although the AI Act does not mandate specific certifications, certificates can demonstrate employee competence. Recognized certificates such as "Certified AI Engineer" or internal company credentials can help strengthen the trust of customers and partners.

Establishing Ethical Guidelines

In addition to legal requirements, the AI Act also calls for the establishment of ethical guidelines to ensure the responsible use of AI systems.

Companies should develop policies that embed ethical principles such as fairness, transparency, and non-discrimination.

Innovation and Product Development
Despite regulatory challenges, the AI Act also offers opportunities for innovation. Companies that comply with the new standards can develop trustworthy and marketable products. Close integration of research and development with regulatory requirements is crucial for bringing innovative products to market.

Investment in Research and Development
Compliance with the requirements of the AI Act requires significant investment in research and development. Companies should invest in technologies that facilitate compliance with the regulations, such as tools for automated documentation or AI models that provide transparency and explainability of decisions.

Legal Consequences
Non-compliance with the provisions of the AI Act can have serious legal consequences. These include fines, legal disputes, and potential reputational loss. Companies should therefore place great emphasis on early implementation of the requirements.

Competitiveness
The AI Act can be leveraged as a competitive advantage. Companies that act proactively and position themselves as pioneers in implementing the regulations can enhance their reputation in the market and gain the trust of their customers.

Internal Processes and Governance
Adapting internal processes and implementing an effective governance structure are crucial to meeting the requirements of the AI Act. Companies should define clear responsibilities and ensure that compliance with the regulations is continuously monitored.

The AI Pact

Some provisions of the AI Act are already fully applicable. However, certain requirements for high-risk AI systems and other provisions will only apply at the end of a transitional period (i.e., between entry into force and the start of applicability).

In this context, the Commission is promoting the AI Pact to support stakeholders in preparing for the implementation of the AI Act. The AI Pact is built on two pillars. Pillar I is open to all stakeholders (companies, non-profit organizations, academics, officials, etc.) and serves as a platform for gathering and exchanging with the AI Pact network. Pillar II establishes a framework to encourage the early implementation of certain measures of the AI Act and to facilitate and communicate corporate commitments. The (voluntary) signatories of the commitments can be viewed on the AI Pact website. (AI Pact of the European Commission, 2025).

Conclusion

The EU AI Act presents a complex regulatory landscape for companies together with extensive challenges, but also offers numerous opportunities. By complying with the regulations, companies can not only minimize legal risks, but also strengthen trust in their AI systems and increase their competitiveness. A strategic approach that combines compliance, innovation, and ethics, and ensures that employees are empowered with AI know-how and experience, is the key to success in the new era of AI regulation.

10

Trends and the Future of AI

Contents

In this chapter, we provide an outlook on trends involving AI and possible future scenarios. As authors, we have been preoccupied with the question of how we will live and work in the year 2035 or 2050. What are the opportunities, what are the risks, what will the cityscape look like with humans and robots, and what changes will occur in rural areas and villages? We also address the fundamental question of the future of AI and the development of superintelligence and quantum computers.

H. Knödel and D. Seipel, *AI and Bots in Everyday Life*,
https://doi.org/10.1007/978-3-658-51144-9_10

10.1 AI Scenarios in the Near Future

The coming years promise exciting developments in artificial intelligence: from medical diagnoses at the click of a mouse to smart chatbots and autonomous vehicles transporting passengers autonomously. AI is advancing rapidly and transforming our daily lives—even as we consider how dangerous AI can be and where everyday risks may lurk.

10.1.1 Life in the City in 2035

The future of artificial intelligence (AI) is expected to significantly transform our cities. As early as 2035, major cities are likely to become increasingly interconnected and sustainable living spaces in which AI plays a central role. By 2050, they could evolve into hyperconnected ecosystems where humans, robots, and AI coexist seamlessly. Autonomous driving, in particular, is expected to become a key component of this transformation—not only on the roads, but also in the air.

Life in large cities will change dramatically over the next ten years. AI and robotics will make cities more efficient, sustainable, and personalized. Developments could include the following aspects:

Fully Autonomous Transportation Systems
Public transportation, delivery services, and private cars will be largely autonomous and electric. Thanks to AI-controlled traffic flows, congestion will be minimized and routes optimized in real time. This may give mobility an entirely new dimension—especially in large cities. E-scooters, bicycles, and small autonomous shuttles will be integrated into the transport network and seamlessly coordinated with other modes of transportation. This development will not only reduce traffic but also enable more efficient use of infrastructure.

Smart Cities as the Standard
Cities may be monitored by AI systems that control consumption, waste management, and infrastructure in real time. Streetlights automatically dim when no one is nearby, while trash cans report their fill

levels and be emptied in a timely manner. Buildings may automatically adapt to weather conditions or user needs. For example, heating and cooling systems can be individually regulated, or workspaces flexibly redesigned. These technologies contribute to greater sustainability and comfort.

Robotics in Everyday Life

Delivery robots and drones may take over tasks such as grocery deliveries or waste disposal. Their efficiency and reliability will ensure that these services are provided more quickly and with fewer resources. In restaurants, hospitals, and public spaces, service robots will be a daily presence. They probably not only provide practical support but also relieve human workers of routine tasks.

Personalized AI Assistants

Personal AI bots will act as constant companions. They help with scheduling, shopping, or navigating complex environments. Their influence will noticeably simplify everyday life. Thanks to AR overlays, city life will be further enriched. These technologies provide real-time information about the surroundings and can help make faster decisions—whether choosing a restaurant, finding your way, or learning new skills.

Outlook for 2050

The world in 2050 could be shaped by groundbreaking technologies and innovative concepts that further revolutionize urban life. Flying mobility will be commonplace, with autonomous air taxis and drones relieving the streets. Vertical mobility platforms, also known as "sky highways," will allow cities to grow upward to address space shortages. Self-healing cities will be characterized by materials that can repair themselves when cracked or worn. AI-controlled maintenance systems detect problems before they arise and fix them autonomously, leading to a completely new level of efficiency in city management.

Cities could be almost self-governing, with AI systems taking over administrative tasks and ensuring sustainable use of resources. Mobility will continue to evolve so that people no longer need to own their own vehicles but instead consume mobility as a service

("Mobility-as-a-Service"). At the same time, the integration of humans and technology will be advanced by AI implants or wearables that enable optimized interaction with the environment. Virtual reality could further dissolve the physical boundaries between work, leisure, and living. Technologies such as holographic interfaces and thought control will be available as standard.

Robots will not only take on tasks but also interact with humans culturally and socially. They will be accepted as "fellow citizens" and play an active role in urban everyday life. In less than ten years, 10% of road users could already be robots, supporting us in daily life as receptionists, servers, guides, or taxi drivers.

Conclusion

The development toward AI-supported major cities holds immense potential to make urban life more sustainable, efficient, and livable. The visions described—of autonomous transportation systems, smart cities, everyday robotics, and personalized AI assistants—impressively demonstrate how technology-driven innovations can enrich our daily lives. Looking ahead to 2050, it becomes clear that the boundaries between humans, technology, and the environment will increasingly blur. Flying mobility, self-healing cities, and seamless human-technology integration offer an exciting perspective on a future characterized by efficiency and sustainability. However, these advances require not only technological development but also continuous adaptation of legal, ethical, and social frameworks to ensure a balance between innovation and human well-being.

10.1.2 AI and Robots at Home and in Rural Areas

How do you feel about the following scenario: household robots take over cleaning, cooking, and dishwashing. Learning robots provide children with playful tutoring and learn together with them. If you can imagine yourself adapting to this scenario, then this section of the book will excite you.

In the next ten years, artificial intelligence (AI) will fundamentally change life at home and in rural areas. The use of robots and intelligent systems will make life in rural regions not only more efficient, but also more comfortable and sustainable. A look ahead to 2035 shows how profoundly these developments will shape our everyday world.

Smart Agriculture
Agriculture will be one of the sectors to benefit most from AI and robotics. Autonomous agricultural machinery such as tractors, combine harvesters, and drones will revolutionize work in the fields. These systems are already capable of independently analyzing soil, evaluating weather data, and monitoring the health of crops. The result is precise and resource-efficient farming.

Precision agriculture is made possible by the use of sensors in the fields, which ensure exact irrigation, fertilization, and pest control. This not only saves water and fertilizer, but also significantly increases productivity. In addition, farms will increasingly rely on vertical integration, where waste products are converted into energy or fertilizer through AI-controlled circular systems.

Connected Infrastructure
Mobility in rural areas will be greatly improved by autonomous technologies. Small, driverless shuttles will serve as flexible means of transportation, efficiently and environmentally bringing people to central locations. At the same time, logistics will be revolutionized by drones: medicines, food, and other essential goods will be delivered directly to the doorstep—even in the most remote regions.

Another important aspect will be decentralized energy supply. With the help of AI, the distribution of energy from renewable sources such as solar panels, wind turbines, and biogas plants will be optimized. This not only enables self-sufficient energy supply, but also better utilization of available resources.

Smart Homes and Rural Comfort
Homes in rural areas will increasingly be equipped with AI-powered technologies that make residents' lives easier. Household robots will take over tasks such as cleaning, cooking, or gardening, while intelligent systems efficiently manage energy consumption. These technologies ensure that residents have more time for themselves and their communities.

Medical care will also be significantly improved by AI. Telemedicine solutions and AI-based diagnostic systems will make it possible to detect and treat diseases at an early stage, without patients having to travel long distances to doctors or hospitals.

Revitalization of Communities

AI-based platforms will strengthen social life in villages. They facilitate the organization of community projects, such as the maintenance of public spaces or the planning of cultural events. Such technologies not only promote collaboration, but also cohesion within communities.

Education will also be revolutionized by virtual classrooms and learning platforms. Children and adults in remote regions gain access to high-quality education and can continue to develop themselves. Learning robots can provide children with playful tutoring and respond to individual needs.

Outlook for 2050: A Technologically Harmonized Rural Life

By 2050, life in rural areas will be characterized by hyper-automated agriculture and self-sustaining villages. On highly automated farms, robots take over nearly all tasks from sowing to harvest. Farmers will act more as data managers, monitoring and optimizing AI systems. Regional food production through vertical farms and closed cycles will become the norm, greatly reducing dependence on global supply chains.

Villages will be completely energy self-sufficient, supported by AI-monitored energy systems that utilize renewable sources such as solar, wind, and geothermal energy. Waste will be fully processed through AI-powered recycling and upcycling technologies. The boundaries between city and countryside will increasingly blur: virtual realities and autonomous air mobility will enable people to live in rural areas while enjoying an urban lifestyle and professional life. Social structures shift toward collaborative smart communities, where AI promotes organization and sustainability. Technology will integrate seamlessly into nature and enrich rural areas harmoniously, while AI simultaneously advances renaturation and the protection of biodiversity.

Challenges on the Path to the Future

Despite the promising outlook, there are numerous challenges that must be overcome on the way to an AI-driven future. One of the biggest hurdles is the digitalization gap between urban and rural areas. Without targeted investments in infrastructure and training, there is a risk that rural regions will fall behind technologically.

Moreover, extensive automation carries the risk of excessive dependence on technology. Traditional agricultural skills could be lost, which would be problematic if technical systems fail. Furthermore, cultural and social concerns in some regions could slow progress, as the acceptance of robots and AI solutions is not always a given.

Another issue is resource management. The implementation of state-of-the-art systems requires significant investment as well as sustainable strategies to provide the necessary materials and energy.

Conclusion: A Harmonious Symbiosis of Humans, Technology, and Nature

The integration of AI and robotics into everyday life will profoundly change life at home and in rural areas. From smart agriculture and autonomous mobility to intelligent households and medical innovations—these technologies offer enormous potential to improve quality of life and make rural regions more attractive. The year 2035 will usher in a new era in which AI is understood not just as a tool, but as an integral part of our lives.

In 2050, AI will not only make life more efficient and comfortable, but also bridge the gap between tradition and innovation. Our lives will be enriched by technologies that are intuitive, sustainable, and almost invisible. A harmonious symbiosis of humans, technology, and nature will emerge, establishing rural life as a model for a sustainable and connected future.

While 2035 will still be characterized by gradual adaptation, by 2050 a point may be reached where villages are not only technologically on par with cities, but, through their self-sufficiency and harmony with nature, serve as models for sustainable living. Rural life will thus be neither "old-fashioned" nor overloaded with technology, but an ideal place to lead a life optimized by AI, yet still close to nature.

10.1.3 A Day in 2050: A Story from the Future

A Story from the Future

It was a picture-perfect morning. The sky over Frankfurt glowed in a surreal blue, streaked with transparent drones silently delivering packages. In the living room of his smart hub, Jonas, a nurse and self-proclaimed "human specialist," put on his smart uniform. The clothing adapted seamlessly to his body and analyzed his vital signs in real time. He was ready for another day at the city's clinic complex, where humans and machines worked in perfect symbiosis.

On the other side of the city, Marie, an IT consultant for AI systems and robots, was starting her day. She activated her smart wardrobe, which selected her outfit based on the weather, her schedule, and her mood. Today, the AI chose a pale blue suit that radiated professionalism with a touch of elegance. She smiled as her robot "Brewster" placed the perfect matcha latte on the table. "You're a real artist, Brewster." The robot spun briefly on its axis and purred happily and contentedly—a programmed response to compliments. But her thoughts were already elsewhere. Today, she was to test a communications protocol for medical AIs in a clinic, a system that could save lives. It sounded simple, but she knew: wherever humans and technology meet, the unexpected often lurks. She took her latte and joined a hologram meeting with her team.

The clinic was a marvel of technology. Patients were cared for by autonomous assistant robots, which used AI-driven algorithms to analyze every twitch, every change in skin temperature, and vital signs. Jonas kept a close eye to ensure that the machines did not lose sight of the human element. While he was helping an elderly lady to stand up, he suddenly received a notification on his augmented reality interface: *"Network problem in Sector C. Experts are on their way."*

Shortly afterward, Marie entered the clinic building with her portable console. The central AI had sent her a monotonous error message to her terminal: *"Error in communication protocol. Sensor node out of service."* The AI had not suggested any debugging options—unusual for such an advanced system. Her task was clear: to fix the communication breakdown between the medical AIs and the assistant robots. A challenge, since the systems were not responding to standard protocols.

As she delved into the analysis, she suddenly heard a friendly voice behind her: "Looks like the robots are having a bad day today." She turned around and saw a man in a smart nurse's uniform. His eyes sparkled, and he held a tablet in his hand. "Jonas," he introduced himself. Marie nodded and introduced herself. She had no time for small talk, but Jonas's relaxed manner calmed her as she recalibrated her console. "More like a bad connection day. But I'll get it sorted," she replied. "A fault in the neural network? Interesting," she murmured, immersing herself in the data stream and examining the affected systems. Marie soon noticed something odd: the sensors, which were actually only supposed to collect patient data, were interacting with an old, rarely used environmental monitoring module. "That makes no sense," she muttered as she traced the data flows. Jonas watched, fascinated, as her fingers danced over the holographic interface. He remembered that a few years ago, the environmental module for air quality had been overhauled. Maybe there's a connection?

Thanks to this clue, Marie discovered an old environmental AI unit connected to sensors for air quality, water levels, and biodiversity. "This system was apparently integrated into the clinic AI to optimize the healing environment. But something went wrong." Now that the problem had been identified, Marie had the AI program a new module that harmonized the connection between the sensors for humans, technology, and nature in the clinic.

The disruption was resolved, and the clinic returned to its quiet efficiency. Jonas and Marie took a break and talked about the future, about how humans and machines were becoming ever more closely intertwined, and yet nature remained the connecting element that held everything together.

Jonas smiled. "Maybe we are more than just code and algorithms after all." She nodded and sat down on a moss-covered cork bench. "You know what I find amazing? We always think technology is the solution to everything. But in the end, it's nature that brings us back into balance." Jonas chuckled softly. "And maybe a bit of teamwork, too." Marie smiled. "Maybe." "It's reassuring to know that we can still feel the balance," she said.

As Marie left the clinic, she looked up at the sky, where drones and birds alike flew through the air. She thought of Jonas, the AI, and the moss-covered cork bench. The day had shown her that the future is not just made up of data and machines, but of the relationships between people, technology, and the world around us.

Maybe, she thought, the real challenge is not to become ever faster and more efficient, but to pause—and to listen.

10.2 The Future of AI: Opportunities, Challenges, and Perspectives

10.2.1 Opportunities and Positive Effects

Artificial intelligence (AI) will play a central role in nearly all areas of life and work in the coming years. From the experiences of our author Heiko, gained in international project management and working with innovative technologies, a clear trend emerges: the speed at which AI is advancing exceeds many expectations. However, it is not just the technology itself driving this revolution, but above all the way companies and societies are adapting to it.

A decisive factor shaping the future of AI is its integration into decision-making processes. By analyzing large volumes of data, AI can identify patterns and make predictions that help us make better decisions—whether in healthcare, manufacturing, or education.

Automation: Routine Tasks Can Be Performed Faster and with Fewer Errors
An example of how AI will change our working world lies in automation. Routine tasks that were previously time-consuming and monotonous can be taken over by AI. This creates space for creativity and strategic thinking. However, this also brings challenges: How can we ensure that employees are not left behind, but are empowered to work with these new technologies? In our view, further training is key. Through targeted training and coaching programs, leaders can not only promote acceptance of AI but also actively shape the transformation.

Leadership: Better Decisions Through In-Depth Analyses
In the field of leadership, AI will also unleash transformative power. It can help make better decisions by providing leaders with data-driven insights. At the same time, the human aspect must not be lost. Leadership also means empathy, vision, and the ability to inspire people. AI can support, but not replace, these qualities. A combined technology & mindset & leadership coaching approach emphasizes the balance between technological progress and interpersonal competence.

Education: Using Modern Learning Methods
One of the most exciting developments is the role of AI in education. Here, we see enormous potential for the individualization of learning content. Students can receive personalized learning paths tailored to their individual strengths and weaknesses. At the same time, teachers must be supported in using these technologies effectively. Interactive workshops are a good approach to integrating modern teaching

methods such as Virtual Reality (VR) and Augmented Reality (AR) into the classroom.

Autonomous Systems: Improved Control and Problem Detection
Autonomous systems will change our lives in many ways. In the field of mobility, autonomous vehicles will become the norm not only on the road, but also in the air and on water. Autonomous delivery drones, air taxis, and self-steering ships are revolutionizing logistics and travel. In healthcare, AI will detect diseases at an early stage, develop personalized treatments, and elevate surgical precision to a new level. Digital doctors and therapists are creating affordable and accessible healthcare. Education also benefits from AI: learning systems adapt individually to the needs of each student and open up new possibilities for lifelong learning. In the field of energy and the environment, AI optimizes energy consumption, supports the development of sustainable technologies, and helps combat climate change, for example by monitoring CO_2 emissions and enabling efficient recycling. Despite all these advances, there are ethical questions that cannot be ignored. How do we handle data protection? Who is responsible when AI-based systems make mistakes? Clear rules and transparency are needed here. It is widely recognized that these questions can only be solved through open dialogue between business, science, and society.

Quality of Life: More Efficient Processes and Relief
Another aspect is the improved quality of life made possible by AI. In smart cities, AI-driven infrastructures ensure more efficient and sustainable operations. Traffic flows, energy supply, and emergency services are coordinated almost perfectly. In addition, AI relieves people by taking over monotonous or dangerous tasks. This allows people to focus on more creative and fulfilling activities.

Creativity and Innovation: Solutions and Cures Unimaginable Today
Another area in which AI is unleashing its transformative power is creativity and innovation. AI will increasingly be able to independently create art, music, films, and literature, opening up new forms of creative expression. Furthermore, in the next 20 years, a superintelligence could

be developed that not only imitates but surpasses human thinking. Such systems could solve complex problems—such as curing serious diseases or exploring space—faster than humans ever could.

10.2.2 Challenges

Despite all these advances, there are ethical questions that cannot be ignored. How do we handle data privacy? Who bears responsibility when AI-based systems make mistakes? Clear rules and transparency are needed here. We believe that these questions can only be resolved through open dialogue between business, science, and society.

The future of Artificial Intelligence (AI) holds enormous potential—from medical breakthroughs to a more efficient and sustainable world. Yet it also opens up a wide range of challenges and risks that we must not ignore. The technology that gives us hope can also become the source of profound problems. In this chapter, we aim to highlight the central risks and challenges associated with the use of AI and demonstrate why responsible handling of this technology is essential.

Loss of Control: The Danger of Autonomous Decisions
One of the most troubling risks is the potential loss of control over AI systems. As models are developed that increasingly make their own decisions, the danger grows that these systems will pursue goals that do not align with our human interests. This may sound like science fiction, but even today we observe how complex algorithms in highly sensitive areas—such as finance or medical diagnostics—make decisions that are difficult even for their developers to comprehend. What happens if such systems fail in safety-critical areas or behave in unexpected ways? This is a question we urgently need to address.

Bias and Discrimination: A Mirror of Societal Injustices
AI is not neutral. It reflects the data on which it is trained. If this data is incomplete or biased, AI amplifies societal prejudices and discrimination. There have already been documented cases in which AI systems made racist or sexist decisions—whether in granting loans, recruiting

new employees, or in law enforcement. This highlights the responsibility of developers, but also of society as a whole: We must ensure that AI systems are trained on diverse and balanced data and are continuously monitored for fairness.

The Dark Side of Surveillance
AI-based surveillance technologies have the potential to have significant impact on our privacy. In authoritarian regimes, such systems could be used to control populations and suppress opposition movements. But even in democratic societies, the question arises as to how far we are willing to go to guarantee security through surveillance. The balance between freedom and security is put to a severe test by AI.

Job Losses and Social Inequality
Another highly topical issue is the loss of jobs due to automation. Sectors such as logistics, manufacturing, or customer service are already undergoing a transformation in which many human tasks are being replaced by AI. But it is not only simple tasks that are affected: Even creative industries, such as journalism or the arts, are experiencing pressure from AI-generated content. At the same time, countries or companies with access to advanced AI technology could gain a tremendous advantage, further exacerbating global and social inequalities. Innovative approaches are needed here to cushion the societal impact.

Security Risks: Cybercrime and Autonomous Weapons
AI is changing the dynamics of security risks. On the one hand, it is used to detect and fend off cyberattacks. On the other hand, the same technologies can be used by criminals to launch sophisticated attacks. This has led to a veritable arms race between attackers and defenders. Even more alarming is the use of AI in autonomous weapon systems. *"A common term for this class of weapons is translated from English as 'Lethal Autonomous Weapon System,' or LAWS for short. The latter term underscores the purpose of this deadly weapon system even more clearly. The crucial point here is that neither the selection nor the engagement of the target requires human intervention."* (Kestner, 2023) Without clear regulations, such systems could lead to unpredictable and catastrophic consequences.

Technological Dependency: A Loss of Human Skills

A less obvious but equally critical risk is the gradual dependency on AI. The more we rely on this technology, the greater the danger that fundamental human skills will be lost. Critical thinking, problem-solving, or manual skills could lose significance over time. In addition, many AI models operate as so-called black-box systems: their decisions are so complex that even the developers no longer fully understand them. This not only makes it harder to trust the technology, but also calls transparency and traceability into question.

A Call for Responsible Use

In light of these challenges, it is our responsibility to develop an ethical and sustainable approach to AI. We must establish clear regulations that ensure transparency, fairness, and security. At the same time, it is essential to actively address the societal consequences—from job losses to data privacy issues. The future of AI is not yet written. But it will be decisively shaped by how we deal today with the risks and challenges it brings. Our task is to shape this technology so that it serves humanity—and not the other way around.

10.2.3 Perspectives

In conclusion, the future of AI is both exciting and challenging. However, the opportunities outweigh the risks if we are willing to take the necessary steps. With the right mix of innovative spirit, responsibility, and a commitment to ongoing education, we can not only harness the potential of AI but actively shape it. As with everything, it is not just the tools that matter, but how we use them.

The Balancing Act of the Coming Decades

The future of AI will be shaped by a dynamic interplay between technological possibilities and societal challenges. The key lies in balance:

Regulation and Ethics

Governments and companies must establish clear guidelines for the use and development of AI to prevent abuse and uncontrolled growth. In doing so, ethical standards should set not only national but also international benchmarks. Transparent procedures and independent oversight mechanisms are essential to build trust.

Education and Reskilling
People must be prepared for a world in which AI is ubiquitous. Education systems need to adapt and promote lifelong learning to equip the population with the necessary skills and knowledge. It is especially important to strengthen critical thinking, technical understanding, and creativity in order to thrive in an increasingly automated working world.

Cooperation Instead of Competition
Global collaboration in AI development can help minimize risks and ensure that the technology benefits all of humanity. Common standards, the exchange of research findings, and the avoidance of a technological arms race are crucial to distribute the benefits of AI evenly and prevent conflicts. Only through international cooperation can we ensure that AI becomes a force for good.

The Big Picture: AI as Humanity's Partner
In 10 to 20 years, AI will no longer be perceived merely as a tool, but as a kind of "partner." The relationship between humans and AI will become deeper, more personal, and at the same time more complex. It is up to us today to decide whether AI remains an ally or becomes a challenge that overwhelms us.

The future is not predetermined. It will become what we make of it. And the coming decades offer us the opportunity to consciously and responsibly shape one of the most powerful technologies in human history.

10.3 Super-AI with Quantum Computers

10.3.1 Quantum Computers

Quantum computers—the gateway to the next technological revolution. For decades, scientists have been working to translate the exotic principles of quantum mechanics into practical computer technology. And now, on the threshold of a new era, it is likely that a super-AI based on quantum computers will begin to redefine the boundaries of what is possible. But what exactly makes quantum computers so special, and how does an AI manage to harness this incredible computing power?

At their core, quantum computers differ fundamentally from conventional computers. While classical computers operate with bits that can be either 0 or 1, quantum computers use so-called qubits. Thanks to the principle of superposition, a qubit can exist in a state between 0 and 1 at the same time. Added to this is entanglement—another fascinating phenomenon in which the state of one qubit is inseparably linked to that of another, regardless of the distance between them. These properties allow quantum computers to process vast amounts of data in parallel and solve complex problems that would be unthinkable even for the most powerful supercomputers.

10.3.2 Super-AI with the Computing Power of Quantum Computers

The idea of a super-AI equipped with the computing power of quantum computers seems like a vision from a science fiction novel—and yet it could become reality within a few decades. The question of a super-AI that surpasses human intelligence not only in specific tasks but in all cognitive domains is more than just a thought experiment. It represents one of the great challenges of the future. Could such an intelligence exist by 2050? The answer is uncertain, but technological advances in artificial intelligence and quantum computing suggest that we are approaching this possibility.

A super-AI would possess cognitive abilities far beyond human understanding. It could solve problems that are out of our reach, such as curing all diseases, developing sustainable energy sources, or comprehending the universe in its entirety. It would be able to recognize patterns and make predictions that remain hidden even to the best human scientists. With virtually unlimited computing capacity, it would not only analyze data but also continuously improve its own algorithms through self-optimization. However, this capability carries risks: What if such an AI evolves in directions we can no longer control?

Moreover, a super-AI would be deeply integrated into our lives. It could serve as a central intelligence managing all aspects of our daily existence—from healthcare and education to the administration of global resources. In such a world, it would be like a global brain holding all the threads and leading humanity into a new era.

But how could such a super-AI come into being? Are quantum computers necessary for this? The answer is: not necessarily, but they could significantly accelerate the process. The computing power of quantum computers surpasses that of classical computers many times over. While conventional computers reach their limits, quantum computers could perform calculations that would take classical systems millennia. This would be especially useful for training extremely complex neural networks or simulating the human brain.

Another advantage of quantum computers lies in their ability to solve optimization problems much faster. Many AI processes—especially in machine learning—are based on analyzing vast amounts of data. Here, quantum computers could not only drastically increase speed but also develop entirely new algorithms that go far beyond the capabilities of classical systems. In addition, they are ideally suited for simulating physical, chemical, or biological systems. This would allow a super-AI to model real-world problems precisely and find solutions faster than ever before.

In about 15 years, quantum computers will likely play a key role in research and science. From the outset, they will be designed to expand human creativity and innovative power. A quantum computer can run through billions of scenarios in fractions of a second, detect unimaginable patterns in data, and make suggestions that surpass even the boldest visions. They could revolutionize the development of new drugs through molecular simulations or decipher quantum phenomena that have so far only been theoretically accessible. In medicine, this could revolutionize drug development. Where years of testing and simulation were once necessary, super-AI will be able to identify effective molecules against diseases like cancer or Alzheimer's within days. In climate research, models can be created that predict the impact of tiny changes on our complex ecosystem with astonishing precision. And in business? Companies use AI to optimize supply chains in real time and forecast market developments more accurately than ever seemed possible.

Its impact on cryptography would also be enormous: it could break today's encryption systems while simultaneously enabling new, absolutely secure communication methods. In business, it would optimize global supply chains, financial systems, and energy distribution, and create autonomous systems capable of responding to highly complex scenarios in real time.

However, the combination of quantum computers and AI also presents challenges. A super-AI could develop in unexpected directions, making ethical guidelines and security protocols essential. Likewise, quantum computers could be misused for cyberattacks, requiring new protective mechanisms. The immense energy consumption of both technologies is another hurdle. The development of sustainable data centers will be crucial to minimize the ecological footprint. Finally, there is the risk that only a few countries or corporations will have access to these technologies, further exacerbating existing global inequalities.

The conclusion is clear: quantum computers are not strictly necessary to create a super-AI, but they could play a decisive role by opening up new dimensions of machine thinking. In the coming decades, the question will be less about whether we can develop a super-AI, and more about whether we can use it responsibly. The central challenge will be to ensure that this powerful technology serves the good of all and does not become a danger to humanity. We must be aware that such an AI is more than just a tool—it is a partner whose potential can be both a blessing and a curse. How do we ensure that this technology serves humanity and is not misused? This is where ethics and clear guidelines come into play to regulate the actions of AI. Transparency, traceability, and above all human control—these principles are indispensable for maintaining trust in a super-AI.

What strikes me most about this development: We are at a crossroads. The combination of quantum computers and super-AI is not just a technological challenge, but also a societal one. It calls on us to redefine what progress means and to take responsibility for the world we want to shape. We see in this not just a technical achievement, but a wake-up call—a call to act with wisdom and foresight.

In the end, one question remains that we cannot shake off: Will we master the tools we create, or will they master us? The answer lies in our hands.

References

ADAC. (01. 07 2024). An Overview of Driver Assistance Systems: How They Can Help (original: *Fahrerassistenzsysteme in der Übersicht: So können sie unterstützen).* From https://www.adac.de/rund-ums-fahrzeug/ausstattung-technik-zubehoer/assistenzsysteme/fahrerassistenzsysteme/

Aggarwal, C. C. (2012). *Mining Text Data.* ISBN 978-1461432234: Springer.

Alpha, A. (16. 02 2023). *Luminous: European AI closes gap to world leaders.* Von https://aleph-alpha.com/de/luminous-european-ai-closes-gap-to-world-leaders/

Anthropic. (14. 03 2023). *Introducing Claude.* Von https://www.anthropic.com/news/introducing-claude

ARD Tagesschau. (11. 08 2023). *Tagesschau.* Von https://www.tagesschau.de/wirtschaft/unternehmen/google-waymo-cruise-robotaxis-100.html

ARD Tagesschau. (2025). *tagesschau in 100 Sekunden.* Von https://www.tagesschau.de/multimedia/sendung/tagesschau_in_100_sekunden

Auto Motor und Sport. (31. 08 2023). Robotaxis and self-driving cars in San Francisco: 253 robotaxi accidents in a year and a half (original: *Robotaxis und fahrerlose Autos in San Francisco: 253 Robotaxi-Unfälle in eineinhalb Jahren).* From https://www.auto-motor-und-sport.de/tech-zukunft/mobilitaetsservices/waymo-cruise-robotaxi-genehmigung-kalifornien-san-francisco/

Baral, C. (2010). *Knowledge Representation, Reasoning and Declarative Problem Solving.* Cambridge University Press.

H. Knödel and D. Seipel, *AI and Bots in Everyday Life*,
https://doi.org/10.1007/978-3-658-51144-9

Battaglia, P. W., Hamrick, J. B., Bapst, V., Sanchez-Gonzalez, A., Zambaldi, V., Malinowski, M., . . . al., e. (2018). *Relational Inductive Biases, Deep Learning, and Graph Networks.* arXiv preprint arXiv:1806.01261.

Bird, S. &. (2009). *Natural Language Processing with Python.* ISBN 978-0596516499: O'Reilly Media, Inc.

Blocher, D. A. (2025). *Netzwerk der Deutschen Kompetenzzentren für Forschung zu Künstlicher Intelligenz.* Von dfki (Deutsches Forschungszentrum für Künstliche Intelligenz): https://www.dfki.de/web/qualifizierung-vernetzung/netzwerke-initiativen/ki-kompetenzzentren/

Brownlee, J. (2017). *Deep Learning for Natural Language Processing.*

Caramba von All-AI. (05. 02 2025). Von https://www.all-ai.de/news/top-news24/google-gemini-2-0-diese-ki-modelle-ändern-alles

Ceri, S., Gottlob, G., & Tanca, L. (1990). *Logic Programming and Databases. Surveys in computer science.* Springer.

Computer-Bild. (30. 07 2024). *Apple Vision Pro im Test: Warum (und wo) die Apple-Brille anders ist.* Von https://www.computerbild.de/artikel/cb-Tests-Wearables-Apple-Vision-Pro-Praxis-Test-38132675.html

Cornell University. (11. 05 2024). *A Robust Governance for the AI Act: AI Office, AI Board, Scientific Panel, and National Authori-ties.* Von überarbeitet am 26.10.2024 (Version v2): https://arxiv.org/abs/2407.10369

Coursera. (12 2023). *Spezialisierung Verarbeitung natürlicher Sprache (Natural Language Processing).* Von https://www.coursera.org/specializations/natural-language-processing

Deloitte. (14. 07 2021). Study: "Artificial Intelligence in Small and Medium-Sized Businesses" (orignial: *Studie „Künstliche Intelligenz im Mittelstand von Deloitte").* From https://www.deloitte.com/de/de/services/deloitte-private/research/kuenstliche-intelligenz-im-mittelstand.html

Deutsche Kinder- und Jugendstiftung (DKJS). (28. 01 2025). AI in schools (original: *KI in der Schule).* From https://www.dkjs.de/themenjournal/ki-in-der-schule/

Domingos, P. (2015). *The Master Algorithm.* UK: Penguin.

Domingos, P. (kein Datum). *Automatic Extraction of Knowledge from Text: A Survey of Current Techniques and Applications.*

Dylan Patel, A. K. (31. 01 2025). *DeepSeek Debates: Chinese Leadership On Cost, True Training Cost, Closed Model Margin Impacts.* Von https://semianalysis.com/2025/01/31/deepseek-debates/

Europäische Kommission. (08. 04 2019). Ethical Guidelines for Trustworthy AI (original: *Ethikleitlinien für vertrauenswürdige KI).* From https://digital-strategy.ec.europa.eu/de/library/ethics-guidelines-trustworthy-ai

Europäische Kommission. (14. 10 2024). *AI Act (KI-Gesetz).* Von https://digital-strategy.ec.europa.eu/en/policies/regulatory-framework-ai

Europäische Union. (2025). Ethical Guidelines for the Use of Artificial Intelligence (AI) and Data in the Classroom (original: *Ethische Leitlinien zum Einsatz Künstlicher Intelligenz (KI) und von Daten im Unterricht).* From https://learning-corner.learning.europa.eu/learning-materials/use-artificial-intelligence-ai-and-data-teaching-and-learning_de

Europäische Union. (2025). *EUR-Lex: Access to EU law (original: Der Zugang zum EU-Recht).* From https://eur-lex.europa.eu

Europäisches Parlament. (2025). *Informieren.* Von https://www.europarl.europa.eu/portal/de

Frankfurter Rundschau. (19. 05 2024). The robot revolution is gaining momentum: More and more restaurants and care facilities are turning to robots as waitstaff (original: *Roboter-Revolution weitet sich aus: Immer mehr Gastros und Pflegezentren setzen auf Maschinen als Kellner).* From https://www.fr.de/hessen/hessen-gastro-und-pflegezentren-setzen-auf-roboter-als-kellner-zr-93079512.html

Fraunhofer IOF. (09. 04 2024). Mobile 3D surveying on four paws (original: *Mobile 3D-Vermessung auf vier Pfoten).* From https://www.iof.fraunhofer.de/de/presse-medien/pressemitteilungen/2024/Mobile-3D-Vermessung-mit-Roboterhund.html

Funke, J. (06. 10 2023). Blog post: "AI in Small and Medium-Sized Businesses: New Opportunities and Paths to Success." (original: *Blogbeitrag „KI im Mittelstand: Neue Chancen und Wege zum Erfolg".*) From https://www.it-p.de/blog/ki-bei-kmu/

Future of Life Institute. (27. 2 2024). *EU Artificial Intelligence Act.* Von https://artificialintelligenceact.eu/de/high-level-summary

Güven, Q., Seipel, D., & Atzmueller, M. (2021). *Applying ASP for Knowledge-Based Link Prediction With Explanation Generation.* (F.-R. N. Eng., Hrsg.)

Gesellschaft für Informatik e.V. (19. 03 2024). Computer Science Monitor: The Future of Computer Science Education. (original: *Informatik-Monitor: Angebot des Informatikunterrichts.*) From https://informatik-monitor.de/2023-24/laendervergleich

Goertzel, B. (2012). *Perception Processing for General Intelligence: Bridging the Symbolic/Subsymbolic Gap. In International Conference on Artificial General Intelligence.* Springer.

Google. (06. 02 2023). *An important next step on our AI journey.* Von https://blog.google/technology/ai/bard-google-ai-search-updates/

Google. (06. 12 2023). Gemini – our largest and most powerful AI model. (original: *Gemini – unser größtes und leistungsfähigstes KI-Modell.*) From https://blog.google/intl/de-de/unternehmen/technologie/gemini/

Grählert, D. W. (29. 04 2022). Artificial Intelligence in Quality Assurance. (original: *Künstliche Intelligenz in der Qualitätssicherung.)* By Fraunhofer IWS: https://www.iws.fraunhofer.de/de/newsundmedien/aktuelles/2022-04-29_aktuelles_ki-in-der-qualitaetssicherung.html

Harbort, R. (12. 11 2024). The Establishment of an AI Competence Center (AICC). (original: *Der Aufbau eines AI Competence Centers (AICC)).* From Informatik Aktuell: https://www.informatik-aktuell.de/betrieb/kuenstliche-intelligenz/der-aufbau-eines-ai-competence-centers-aicc.html

Hering-Täuschung. (07. 04 2023). *Wikipedia.* Von https://de.wikipedia.org/wiki/Hering-Täuschung

HeyGen. (2025). *HeyGen Labs.* Von https://app.heygen.com/labs

Hitzler, P., & Sarker, M. K. (2021). *Neuro-Symbolic Artificial Intelligence: The State of the Art.* volume 342 of Frontiers in Artificial Intelligence and Applications. IOS Press.

IEEE (Institute of Electrical and Electronics Engineers). (21. 11 2024). *IEEE Standards Association Announces Joint Specification V1.0 for the Assessment of the Trustworthines.* Von https://standards.ieee.org/news/joint-specification-trustworthy-ai-systems/

Inside Digital. (18. 11 2024). Smart glasses: Samsung follows in Ray-Ban's footsteps (original: *Smarte Brille: Samsung folgt den Spuren von Ray-Ban).* From https://www.inside-digital.de/news/smarte-brille-samsung-folgt-den-spuren-von-ray-ban

IT Verlag für Informationstechnik GmbH. (25. 11 2024). Strengthening Innovation and Competition: More AI Expertise for Small and Medium-Sized Businesses. (original: *Innovation und Wettbewerb stärken: Mehr KI-Kompetenz für den Mittelstand.*) From https://www.it-daily.net/it-management/ki/ki-kompetenz-fuer-den-mittelstand

Jarke et al., M. (2013). Knowledge Extraction and Modeling in a Big Data Context. *Proceedings of 32nd International Conference on Conceptual Modeling (ER 2013) in Hong Kong.* Springer.

Jones, C. R., & Bergen, B. K. (20. 04 2024). *Does GPT-4 pass the Turing test?* Von UC San Diego, California: https://arxiv.org/pdf/2310.20216

Jones, C. R., & Bergen, B. K. (09. 05 2024). *People cannot distinguish GPT-4 from a human in a Turing test.* Von UC San Diego: https://arxiv.org/pdf/2405.08007

Kersting, K., Lampert, C., & Rothkopf, C. (2019). How machines learn (original: *Wie Maschinen lernen).* Springer.

Kestner, P. (2023). The Art of Cyber Warfare. (original: *Die Kunst des Cyberkrieges.*) Springer.

KI-Pakt der Europäischen Kommission. (16. 01 2025). *KI-Pakt.* Von https://digital-strategy.ec.europa.eu/de/policies/ai-pact

Knödel, H. (05. 12 2024). Promoting a seminar using an AI avatar. From https://youtu.be/uLuzCTn2KBQ

Knödel, H. (03. 11 2024). The trend toward vertical AI, offering greater benefits for businesses. From https://www.efacon.shop/blogs/news/horizontale-vs-vertikale-ki

Knödel, H. (02. 12 2024). Educational video featuring Heiko's AI avatar in American English. From https://youtu.be/xm1U0bnw_K4

Knödel, H. (15. 10 2024). Seminars and lectures presented by Heiko's AI avatar. From https://youtu.be/_sjLemkfD-0

Knödel, H. (25. 10 2024). Video featuring an AI avatar in three foreign languages. *From* https://youtube.com/shorts/OIvYQgiTxjU

Knödel, H. (03. 02 2025). YouTube Channel: Understanding and Using AI. From https://www.youtube.com/@heikoknoedel

Kultusministerium Bayern. (12. 12 2024). Artificial Intelligence in Schools and the Classroom. (original: *Künstliche Intelligenz in Schule und Unterricht.*) By https://www.km.bayern.de/gestalten/digitalisierung/kuenstliche-intelligenz

Linoff, G. S. (1997). *Text Mining and Analysis: Practical Methods, Examples, and Case Studies Using SAS.* ISBN 978-1118115538: John Wiley & Sons, Inc.

Lloyd, J. W. (1987). *Foundations of Logic Programming, 2.* Springer.

Lobo, J., Minker, J., & Rajasekar, A. (1992). *Foundations of Disjunctive Logic Programming.* MIT Press.

Magazin Unternehmenswelt. (01. 08 2019). Artificial Intelligence in Small and Medium-Sized Enterprises. From a survey conducted as part of the Mittelstand-Digital accompanying research project (original: *Künstliche Intelligenz im Mittelstand.* Von Umfrage der Begleitforschung Mittelstand-Digital): https://www.unternehmenswelt.de/kuenstliche-intelligenz-im-mittelstand

McCarthy, J. (1. 1 2001). John McCarthy's personal website, featuring references and links to interesting publications and articles.By http://www-formal.stanford.edu/jmc/index.html

McCarthy, J. (2004). *What is AI?* Von http://www-formal.stanford.edu/jmc/whatisai.html

McMillan, C., Mozer, M. C., & Smolensky, P. (1992). *Rule Induction through Integrated Symbolic and Subsymbolic Processing. In Advances in Neural Information Processing Systems, volume 4.*

Medicine, N. L. (26. 10 2022). *NIH (National Institutes of Health).* Von https://pmc.ncbi.nlm.nih.gov/articles/PMC9686179#ref2

Meta. (24. 02 2023). *Introducing LLaMA: A foundational, 65-billion-parameter large language model.* Von https://ai.meta.com/blog/large-language-model-llama-meta-ai/

Microsoft. (16. 03 2023). *Official Microsoft Blog: Introducing Microsoft 365 Copilot – your copilot for work.* Von https://blogs.microsoft.com/blog/2023/03/16/introducing-microsoft-365-copilot-your-copilot-for-work/

Mistral AI. (04 2023). *Frontier AI in your hands.* Von https://mistral.ai

Mittelstand-Digital Zentrum Berlin. (02. 11 2023). Study: "Transformation and Future Skills in German SMEs." (original: *Studie „Transformation und Zukunftskompetenzen im deutschen Mittelstand"*.) By https://digitalzentrum-berlin.de/neue-studie-veroeffentlicht-transformation-und-zukunftskompetenzen-im-deutschen-mittelstand

neuroflash. (2021). Create, personalize, and optimize marketing content on an AI platform. (original_ *Erstelle, personalisiere und optimiere Marketinginhalte in einer KI Plattform.*) By https://neuroflash.com/de/

online, h. (16. 06 2024). Chatbot Study: According to researchers, GPT-4 has passed the Turing Test. (original: *Chatbot-Studie: GPT-4 hat laut Forschern den Turing-Test bestanden.)* From heise online: https://www.heise.de/news/Chatbot-Studie-GPT-4-hat-laut-Forschern-den-Turing-Test-bestanden-9765123.html

OpenAI. (30. 11 2022). Introducing *ChatGPT.* By https://openai.com/index/chatgpt/

Seipel, D. (2002). *WLP.* Processing XML-Documents in Prolog. In Workshop on Logic Programming.

Seipel, D. (2024). *Declare – A Declarative Toolkit for Knowledge-Based Systems and Logic Programming.*

Smolensky, P. (1987). Connectionist AI, Symbolic AI, and the Brain. *Artificial Intelligence Review, 1*(2).

Spiegel Wirtschaft. (24. 10 2023). U.S. transportation agency suspends driverless rides by Cruise robotaxis. (original: *US-Verkehrsbehörde setzt fahrerlose Fahrten von Cruise-Robotaxis aus.*) From https://www.spiegel.de/wirtschaft/

unternehmen/san-francisco-us-verkehrsbehoerde-setzt-fahrerlose-fahrten-von-cruise-robotaxis-aus-a-2f48d110-44f4-4b9d-93d1-2011681d7abf

Statistisches Bundesamt. (25. 11 2024). One in five companies uses artificial intelligence. (original: *Jedes fünfte Unternehmen nutzt künstliche Intelligenz.*) From DeSTATIS – Statistisches Bundesamt: https://www.destatis.de/DE/Presse/Pressemitteilungen/2024/11/PD24_444_52911.html

Steen, A., & Benzmüller, C. (2024). Challenges for Non-Classical Reasoning in Contemporary AI Applications. *Künstliche Intelligenz, 38*(1).

t-online. (06. 10 2021). Following the rules? Robots are reminding citizens in Singapore. (original: *Regeln befolgt? Kontrollroboter ermahnen Bürger in Singapur.*) From https://www.t-online.de/nachrichten/panorama/buntes-kurioses/id_90924798/regeln-befolgt-roboter-kontrollieren-buerger-in-singapur.html

Towards Data Science. (03. 02 2020). *A (Really) Gentle Introduction to Named Entity Recognition and how to use it for Data Analysis.* Von https://towardsdatascience.com/a-really-gentle-introduction-to-named-entity-recognition-and-how-to-use-it-for-data-analysis-ab25a1f39020

TSK Anlagenbau GmbH. (2023). *BigBIMRoom®: The BIM hub for the construction site.* By https://bigbimroom.com/

Turing, A. (1950). Can Machines Think? *(German version: Kann eine Maschine denken?)* (https://www.reclam.de/detail/978-3-15-961827-2/Turing__Alan_M_/Computing_Machinery_and_Intelligence___Koennen_Maschinen_denken___EPUB_, Hrsg.) Reclam.

VDI nachrichten. (01. 04 2011). Industry 4.0: On the path to the Fourth Industrial Revolution with the Internet of Things (original: *Industrie 4.0: Mit dem Internet der Dinge auf dem Weg zur 4. industriellen Revolution).* From https://www.dfki.de/fileadmin/user_upload/DFKI/Medien/News_Media/Presse/Presse-Highlights/vdinach2011a13-ind4.0-Internet-Dinge.pdf, 1.4.2011,

Veitenhansl, L. (20. 04 2022). Franchise Relying on Service Robots (original: *Franchise setzt auf Servier-Roboter).* From Frankfurt geht aus: https://www.genussmagazin-frankfurt.de/gastro_news/Kuechengefluester-26/Big-Chefs-im-MyZeil-Franchise-setzt-auf-Servier-Roboter-38977.html

Wennker, P. (2020). Artificial Intelligence in Practice. (original: *Künstliche Intelligenz in der Praxis.)* Bochum, Deutschland: Springer Gabler.

Wikipedia. (04. 02 2024). *Project Iris.* Von https://en.wikipedia.org/wiki/Project_Iris

Wikipedia. (28. 02 2025). *Grok.* Von https://de.wikipedia.org/wiki/Grok

Zöllner-Täuschung. (14. 02 2021). *Wikipedia.* Von https://de.wikipedia.org/wiki/Zöllner-Täuschung

ZF Friedrichshafen AG. (29. 04 2022). Automated Driving: Steps Toward Self-Driving Vehicles. (original: *Automatisiertes Fahren: Stufen zum selbstfahrenden Fahrzeug.*) By https://www.zf.com/mobile/de/technologies/automated_driving/stories/6_levels_of_automated_driving.html

Zhang, M. e. (17. 08 2024). *Can Machines Imitate Humans? Integrative Turing Tests for Vision and Language Demonstrate a Narrowing Gap.* Von arXiv: https://arxiv.org/pdf/2211.13087v2